Grow Long, Blessed Night

Grow Long, Blessed Night

Love Poems from Classical India

Martha Ann Selby

OXFORD
UNIVERSITY PRESS
2000

OXFORD
UNIVERSITY PRESS

Oxford New York
Athens Auckland Bangkok Bogotá Buenos Aires Calcutta
Cape Town Chennai Dar es Salaam Delhi Florence Hong Kong
Istanbul Karachi Kuala Lumpur Madrid Melbourne Mexico City Mumbai
Nairobi Paris São Paulo Shanghai Singapore Taipei Tokyo Toronto Warsaw
and associated companies in
Berlin Ibadan

Published by Oxford University Press, Inc.
198 Madison Avenue, New York, New York, 10016

Library of Congress Cataloging-in-Publication Data

Selby, Martha Ann.
Grow long, blessed night: love poems from classical India /
Martha Ann Selby. p. cm.
Includes bibliographical references and index.
ISBN 0-19-512733-1 (cloth : alk. paper)—ISBN 0-19-512734-X (pbk : alk. paper)
1. Love poetry, Indic—Translations into English. 2. Indic poetry—To 1500.
3. Indic poetry (English)
PK2978.E5 S44 2000
891'.2100803543–dc21
00-020193

1 3 5 7 9 8 6 4 2

Printed in the United States of America
on acid-free paper

for Addie and Dwight
Long may they wave

Contents

Acknowledgments

❖ Funding for my research in India was provided by the U.S. Department of Education through a Fulbright-Hays fellowship and by the American Institute of Indian Studies, with additional support from the Committee on Southern Asian Studies at the University of Chicago and from the Mrs. Giles Whiting Foundation. I am very grateful to the above institutions for supporting me and my work, and I would like to thank Geeta Nayar, Kaye Hill, Shirley Payne, and Katherine Mosely for their efficiency and friendship. A timely grant from the University Research Council at Southern Methodist University enabled me to accept a residency at the British Centre for Literary Translation, University of East Anglia, Norwich, during the summer of 1997. I produced many of the translations from the Old Tamil anthology *Aiṅkuṟunūṟu* while in residence there, and I would like to thank Christine Wilson, Terry Hale, and Wolfgang Kukulies for a fun and phenomenally productive month.

A condensed version of chapter 5 was published as an article titled "Desire for Meaning: Providing Contexts for Prākrit *Gāthās*" in *The Journal of Asian Studies* 55, 1 (February 1996). A few of the translations in part 2 of this book have appeared in other sources, including *World Poetry: An Anthology of Verse from Antiquity to Our Time* (Norton, 1998), *The Norton Anthology of World Masterpieces,* expanded sixth edition (Norton, 1996), *Comparative Criticism* 16 (Cambridge University Press, 1994), *Sulfur Magazine* 33, *The Gift of Tamil: Translations from Tamil Literature in Honor of K. Paramasivam,* Norman Cutler and Paula Richman, eds. (Manohar 1992), *Indian Literature* 34, 5 and 30, 1, and in *Nimrod* 31, 2.

This book was made by many, and I would like to thank all the scholars, poets, and friends—many of my helpmates belong to all three categories—for their tremendous support and encouragement during my research and writing. First of all, I would like to thank certain members of the faculty at the University of Chicago for their guidance and suggestions. My mentor and friend, Wendy Doniger, has been a constant source of encouragement, and I would like to thank her for her dazzling comparative insights, for her inspiring energy, and for spiriting me back to the center whenever I wandered down tangential paths. I owe a great deal to Sheldon Pollock, my *ādi-guru,* for his early guidance and for being the first to introduce me to the Sanskrit language and classical Indian literature. My thanks also go to Norman Cutler for his incisive and respectful readings of early drafts, for instilling in me a love for Tamil and Tamilnadu, and for his warm and sustaining friendship. I would also like to thank Ronald Inden for his constant support, loyalty, and darkling wit, and for never failing to tell me even the most difficult truths. Thanks are also due to Paul Friedrich and the late A. K. Ramanujan for their invaluable comments on my translations, and to Donald Justice, who first invited me to try my hand at literary translation, when I was his student at the University of Iowa so long ago.

In India, I was very fortunate to have read the Sanskrit and Prākrit anthologies and commentaries with S. S. Janaki, Adviser, Kuppuswami Sastri Research Institute, Ceṉṉai. Her brilliance, as well as the depth and breadth of her linguistic and cultural knowledge, will forever serve as an inspiration. She died just as I was completing this book, leaving me and several generations of scholars who worked closely with her feeling orphaned and depleted. It is my hope that this book might live up to her standards. R. N. Sampath, former head of the Sanskrit Department at Madras Presidency College, guided my readings of Sanskrit literary *śāstras* with great style and jocularity, and I am grateful to him for sharing with me his profound knowledge of these texts. I would also like to thank the many people staffing the Kuppuswami Sastri Research Institute and the Adyar Library and Research Centre for cheerfully and efficiently helping me locate texts and materials. I wish to acknowledge my profound debt to the late K. Paramasivam for reading Tamil texts and commentaries with me during my two stays in Madurai. His learning, warmth, and humor are greatly missed.

I would like to thank the following friends for their unwavering support and affection throughout the course of my endeavors: Daud Ali, Nadine Berardi, Lyn Bigelow, Joanne Brown, Lawrence Cohen, Elaine Craddock, Faisal Fatehalli Devji, Vinay Dharwadker, Joan Erdman, Patricia Gossman, Ginette Ishimatsu, David Joseph, Linda Levine, Richard Levy, Arvind Krishna Mehrotra, Diane Paull Mines, Sandra King Mulholland, Isabelle and Penelope Nabokov, Catherine O'Harra, Dorothy May Pownall, S. Ramakrishnan, Sudipta and Devika Sen, Sagaree Sengupta, Swami Sevananda, Roxanne Sexauer, Mrs. P. Shenbagavalli, David Shulman, Lee Weissman, and Ruth and Quentin Young.

I am indebted to the many friends in Dallas who supported me throughout the final revisions of this book, especially to Susan Branson, Mark Heller, and Kaitlin Heller, who provided me with literal and metaphorical shelter and sustenance during a hot and difficult summer. I would particularly like to thank Anne Findley for teaching me profound lessons in loyalty and feminism—her steady and steadying friendship will never be forgotten. Thanks are also due to my good friend Rick Halperin, whom I credit for jump-starting my long-dormant political activism and for reminding me of what is truly important.

Finally, my thanks go to Robert and Margaret Nady for bringing India to Nevada, Iowa, and to my father, Victor Selby, and brothers Robert and Richard for never visibly flinching. This book is dedicated with my deepest love to my daughter, Addie Mae West, who has made untold sacrifices on my behalf, and to her partner, Dwight Hinson. Addie's forgiveness and patience are my greatest boons.

Martha Ann Selby

Grow Long, Blessed Night

They say that my donkey-hearted lover
might leave home tomorrow.

Grow long, Blessed Night,
so that for him
tomorrow just won't be.

(Gāthāsaptaśatī 1.46)

Part One

ESSAYS

1

Introduction

This book has been organized so that it may be read in a number of different ways, for there are as many ways to read poems as there are readers of poetry. Ideally, I would prefer that my readers read the *entire* book from start to finish. But if you are the sort of reader who prefers to experience a poem for the first time on your very own terms, then I advise you to stop here and turn immediately to my translations. Or if you are a reader who is interested in poetry from only one of the three traditions represented within these pages, you can match the appropriate essay with the poems that it discusses.

However, I have written and organized this book with a specific goal in mind. The essays contained in part 1 are to serve as a guide to the poems in part 2, with the hope that readers can develop an approximate sense of what it may have been like to have heard them or read them as connoisseurs. The poems themselves have been organized according to a "conversational" convention that is accepted by readers and writers in all three languages. Each poem is keyed by text and source language, and I encourage my readers to "appreciate" these poems in ways that are the most consonant with their individual readerly habits and aesthetic sensibilities.

These introductory essays examine issues of form, figure, and mood in what we now call classical Indian love poetry. My use of the word "classical" reflects the value placed on these poems by the traditions to which they belong. Relatively speaking, the anthologies of poems with which I am concerned *do* come from an "early" time.

The poems that compose the Sanskrit *Amaruśataka,* arguably the latest of these collections, were probably first gathered into an anthology at some point during the seventh or eighth century C.E.[1] The poems from the Tamil anthologies are thought to have been composed in the first few centuries of the Common Era but were not anthologized until hundreds of years later.[2] Legend has it that the Prākrit *Gāthāsaptaśatī* was anthologized by a king of the Sātavāhana dynasty, Hāla, during his brief reign in the early decades of the first century C.E.[3] Therefore, the word "classical" in the Indian context covers a time frame that extends beyond ten centuries and across three languages. It encompasses various modes of text production, assuming that these poems existed for some time before they were chosen for inclusion in the bodies of literature that we now know. By this very inclusion, the poems were already considered "classical" in the sense that they were culled from vast numbers of verses and were carefully selected in nearly every case by a king or a connoisseur of poetry attached to a court.

There is a Prākrit couplet that illustrates this point beautifully. *Gāthāsaptaśatī* 1.3 reads:

> Kind to poets, Hāla,
> from the midst of a crore of *gāthās,*
> collected seven hundred,
> ornamented with figures of speech.[4]

Though the use of the word "crore" is hyperbolic, this same notion exists in the legends that surround the composition of the Tamil poems. Traditional scholars view the extant verses as representative parts of the *kaṭai-c-caṅkam,* the "latter academy," that existed for 1,850 years and was located in Madurai.[5] There were also "middle" and "first" *caṅkam* periods, existing for 3,700 and 4,440 years, respectively. The works of 8,149 poets from these first two *caṅkam* periods are said to have been lost in great floods. Hyperbole notwithstanding, it is clear that what has survived the effects of climate, insects, human carelessness, and religious prejudice is, sadly, very small in comparison to what must have existed at one time.

The Comparative Problem

My analyses will be largely comparative: "Indocentric" but intercultural and translinguistic. First, the purpose of these analyses is to arrive at a "Pan-Indian" sense of what a classical lyric poem is through an exploration of *differences* in these traditions and what they might tell us about the specifics of poetic technique and interpretation. I grant that there are superficial and structural similarities in many of these poems and that, at times, certain figures of speech, similes, metaphors, symbolic systems, terms of address, and various other conventions are strikingly similar, indeed. However, a more satisfying way to address the problem is through a thorough examination of how these apparently similar symbologies are read and interpreted differently, not just by each literary establishment but throughout history. Interpretation is based on a definable agenda. Some of these interpretive agendas may be sectarian; others may be based solely on what the "historical interpreter" perceives and states to be the "function" or the "use" of a particular body of literature.

Second, I am keenly interested in what might be learned about images of men and women and their environmental, political, and sexual worlds, no matter how much these worlds may be confined to the literary imagination. This book will explore ways in which the various "readings" of these texts through history might reflect interrelationships of textuality, gender, and sexuality, and will suggest ways in which these issues can be meaningfully discussed.

As Earl Miner has written, "Some presumption of difference is fundamental to the whole enterprise of comparative literature and to historical understanding,"[6] and, through highlighting these differences, perhaps we will arrive at a definition of the classical Indian lyric not as one large and all-encompassing notion, but as a highly articulated system of genres and sub-genres. I want to compare not just texts but also the literary establishments that produced them.

Previous attempts have tried to identify commonalities. The so-called influence studies conducted by K. S. Srinivasan and George Hart are, in my view, unconvincing and unsuccessful in varying degrees. In his book *The Ethos of Indian Literature: A Study of Its*

Romantic Tradition (New Delhi: Chanakya Publications, 1985), K. S. Srinivasan (a recipient of the Jawaharlal Nehru Fellowship, given only to people who are researching issues that will help reinforce the Indian government's policies on "national integration") is admittedly in search of something he calls "Indianness." The book is naive in its attempts to show that the southern Vindhya mountains were no impediment to cultural exchange and that evidence for this can be found in the poems. His arguments are not necessarily wrong, but they are certainly superficial. Srinivasan is so caught up in the Indian government's attempt to define itself as a "single nation" that he seems to have been blinded to the more subtle nuances involved when engaged in the comparative enterprise.

George L. Hart does a far better job in his sensitive and influential book, *The Poems of Ancient Tamil: Their Milieu and Their Sanskrit Counterparts* (Berkeley: University of California Press, 1975). Hart suggests that Tamil elements may have filtered northward through the membrane of Prākrit *gāthās,* but, unfortunately, he has overlooked facts that challenge many of his theories. Paul Dundas has correctly pointed out that while

> the similarities between Tamil imagery and that of the *Gāthāsaptaśatī* are indeed striking, . . . it would be unwise . . . to assign an exclusively Dravidian provenance to themes and symbols which occur for the first time in Indo-Aryan literature in the *Gāthāsaptaśatī*, for there are many aspects of Tamil poetry which are clearly of northern origin. Moreover, Hart's attempt to show that the *āryā* meter in which the *Gāthāsaptaśatī* is written is Dravidian cannot be supported, since the history of the *āryā* in its earliest forms . . . can be traced to the oldest portions of the Jaina Canon, thus guaranteeing the meter's northern origin.[7]

There is definite evidence in the poems themselves that later Sanskrit poems were inspired by earlier poems in Prākrit. But there is no clear intertextual evidence indicating that Tamil literature influenced the Prākrit (or Sanskrit) compositions in any way whatsoever, though I would suggest a possible relationship between early Prākrit *gāthās* and the short, almost aphoristic verses of the fourth-century Tamil anthology *Aiṅkuṟunūṟu*.

One of the many reasons why the *Gāthāsaptaśatī* is of such interest is that some of the poems of the *Amaruśataka* are clearly Sanskrit recompositions of Prākrit couplets. I am by no means the first reader of these poems to notice this phenomenon. In the introduction to his 1951 edition of the *Śṛṅgāramañjarī* of Saint Akbar Shah, Sanskrit scholar V. Raghavan says:

> Of poetical works, Hāla's *Gāthāsaptaśatī* leads both by chronology and importance. It is a storehouse of verses depicting a large variety of moods, situations, and characters in love. . . . As has been shown in the introduction to its 1933 edition issued by the Nirnaya Sagar Press, as also in the footnotes in the *Amaruśataka* published by the same press, some of the verses of the *Amaruśataka* are directly based on verses in this Prākrit collection.[8]

In this 1933 edition of the *Gāthāsaptaśatī*, editor and commentator Mathurānāth Śāstrī has indeed devoted a portion of his Sanskrit introduction to this very problem. He has pointed to specific instances in which certain images and tropes from the Prākrit *gāthās* have been transposed into the quatrains of the *Amaruśataka*,[9] leading me to hazard the opinion that much of the later erotic poetry in Sanskrit might even be considered a legitimate sub-genre, reworked and elaborately embroidered, of erotic verse in Māhārāṣṭrī.

Here are two poems in which certain boundaries are employed as a trope, the first from the *Gāthāsaptaśatī*, the second from the *Amaruśataka*. For now, this set can serve as an example that indicates that some of the *gāthās* were certainly reworked into Sanskrit:

Forget about the precious sight
of my lover's face
that steals away my heart.
Just seeing the borders
of the fields on the borders
of her village
gives me instant joy.

(*Gāthāsaptaśatī* 2.68)

When my heart was obsessed with her
from love at first sight
and I thought of a way to win her,

when my passion skyrocketed
and the need for a go-between
became greater and greater,

never mind the pleasure I'd get
from eagerly embracing that woman.

Just roaming the streets near her house
evokes supreme delight.

(*Amaruśataka* 100, Arjunavarmadeva's recension)

It is not enough to say that these two bodies of poetry shared motifs. If we look at the poems in their original languages, it is easy to see that the Sanskrit poet has taken the second line of the Prākrit *gāthā* and has further elaborated on the scenario (in both cases, that of a *nāyaka*, or "hero," who is confiding in a male companion). The last line of the Prākrit couplet reads *tag-gāma-chetta-sīmā vi jhatti diṭṭhā suhāveī*, while the last line of the Amaru poem reads *tad-geha-upānta-rathyā-bhramaṇam-api parāṃ nirvṛtiṃ saṃtanoti*, a reworked, urbanized version of the Prākrit line: there is a subtle change from the "rural" to the "urban"; the *gāthā* speaks of borders of fields and villages, while the Sanskrit poem is talking of city streets and houses. The Sanskrit poem is also made much more complex from a metrical point of view. In fact, I suspect that the exigencies of *sragdharā* meter[10] are what make this poem a rather poor one in comparison to the *gāthā*.

The main problem concerning these three groups of poems that I will address in the body of this book is one of interpretation. This is the realm in which the most interesting, and heretofore unexplored, comparative problems lie. I will develop short histories of various "readings" of South Asian classical texts for each language group: Old Tamil, Sanskrit, and Māhārāṣṭrī Prākrit. I will base my ideas on the ways in which poems from these texts have been used in works on poetics to illustrate form, figure, and mood, employing the three most important critical notions from Indian classical poetics as described by traditional scholars: *tiṇai* for Old Tamil, *rasa* for Sanskrit, and *dhvani* for Prākrit.[11] Though this arrangement may seem anachronic to some, I have decided on this particular sequence of languages (which is not based on the chronological order of the particular texts in question but rather on the chronology of the critical ideas that have primarily been used to interpret the texts). I will begin my analyses from the rhetorical standpoint of the ways in which meaning is created by poets and conveyed in their poems. I will then focus on another type of interpretation, the commentary, a genre of writing that is more concerned, in most instances, with *what* poems mean than with the rhetorical mechanics of *how* meaning is produced. In every case, the commentaries—some of them modern—are later in date than the texts on poetics.

The Tamil Corpus

The primary bodies of work that I have chosen for examination are three Tamil anthologies, *Naṟṟiṇi, Kuṟuntokai,* and *Aiṅkuṟunūṟu;* the Sanskrit *Amaruśataka* and a few additional poems from the *Subhāṣitaratnakoṣa;* and the *Gāthāsaptaśatī* and a sprinkling of verses from the *Vajjālagga,* both composed in Māhārāṣṭrī Prākrit.

The Tamil anthologies were composed in the *akam,* or "interior," genre, which, like all the poems I have selected, have the topic of love as their subject. *Naṟṟiṇai* is traditionally accepted as being the earliest of the Tamil anthologies. Its title simply means "Good Landscape" (*nal* = "good"; *tiṇai* = "landscape," "poetic situation"; "context"). It contains 400 poems ascribed to 175 poets. The verses range in length from eight to thirteen lines. The compiler remains anonymous, but the anthology was completed under the patronage of a Pāṇṭiya king, Paṉṉāṭu tanta Pāṇṭiyaṉ Māṟaṉ Vaḻuti, who composed verses 97 and 301 in the collection.[12] Linguistically speaking, there is hardly a single Sanskrit loanword in the entire collection, which might account for the fact that it has been identified as the earliest in date. However, this chronological placement is highly problematic. Although there is an unwavering traditional order in the list, there is no accounting for the fact that some poets (ostensibly the same historical authors) have verses in all the anthologies. The collections themselves are organized on the principle of line length, as most of their titles suggest.

The second anthology, *Kuṟuntokai,* is accepted as the second earliest in date.[13] (There are significantly greater numbers of Sanskrit loanwords in the text.) The title, which means "A Collection of Short Verse," reflects the length of the poems, which are four to nine lines long. The compiler is named in the colophon as Pūrikkō, about whom nothing is known. There is no patron mentioned.

The *Aiṅkuṟunūṟu,* the third anthology in my discussion here, is a fourth-century anthology consisting of five groups of one hundred poems each. Its title literally means "The Short Five Hundred" or "Five Hundred Short Poems." The poems vary from three to six lines in length. Each century focuses on one of the five *tiṇais,* or "landscapes," of reciprocal love prescribed by the *Tolkāppiyam,* an ancient work on Tamil phonology, grammar, and poetics. The anthology itself was commissioned by a Cēra dynasty king, Yāṉai-k-kaṭ Cēy Māntaraṇ Cēral Irumpoṟai. The actual compiler is identified in the colophon as Pula-t-tuṟai Muṟṟiya Kūṭalūr Kiḻār. This text is unique in that it presents the work of only five poets. Each poet composed one hundred poems on the poetic landscape in which he was considered a virtuoso.

As a whole, the *caṅkam* anthologies were rediscovered by U. Vē. Cāminātaiyar (1855–1942) in the late nineteenth century, as he relates in his autobiography, *Eṉ Carittiram* ("My Story"). Cāminātaiyar's discovery of these texts did more than simply recover lost works of literature—it restored a sense of history and of ancient culture to the Tamils in the Dravidian South, spurring a movement of intellectual activity that is now referred to as the "Tamil renaissance." Drawing his inspiration from, among other things, an English-language biblical concordance, Cāminātaiyar edited the anthologies and wrote lucid commentaries on them. Taking his cue from parts of an old commentary on the *Puṟanāṉūṟu,*[14] he adopted the notions of *tiṇai* ("context") and *tuṟai* ("theme") and transformed them into critical tools. *Tiṇai* and *tuṟai* are, for all practical purposes, archetypal ideas that are unique to early Tamil intellectual paradigms as first set out in the *Tolkāppiyam.* The very name of this text denotes its antiquity as well as its importance: *Tol-kāppiyam* simply means "the old text," though Tamil nationalist scholars offer a different derivation for the word *kāppiyam.* Refusing to accept *kāppiyam* as a

Tamilized form of the Sanskrit word *kāvya* ("text," "poem," "work"), they derive it from the phrase *kāppu iyaṉṟatu,* "that which constitutes protection," the idea being that grammar is what protects language from deterioration.

There is still a great deal of controversy surrounding the date of this text. Both Kamil Zvelebil and K. Paramasivam have developed convincing but conflicting arguments. Zvelebil places the*Tolkāp-piyam* in two periods, dividing the text into two strata, the Ur-*Tolkāp-–piyam* (containing the first two sections on phonology and syntax) and the *Poruḷatikāram,* which comprises the section on rhetoric, poetics, and usage. He placed the composition of the Ur-text at around the second century B.C.E. and the *Poruḷatikāram* some seven centuries later.[15] Paramasivam has argued on linguistic and stylistic grounds that the *Tolkāppiyam* could only have been written by one author and that its composition must have preceded the extant *cañkam* anthologies. He places the entire text in the second century B.C.E.,[16] making it roughly contemporaneous with the composition of the earliest segments of the Sanskrit *Nāṭyaśāstra,* the earliest known work in Sanskrit on dramaturgy and, by extension, poetics. However, Takanobu Takahashi provides us with what I think are the most reasonable dates for the *Tolkāppiyam.* In his recent book, he puts forth a very sensible and concise discussion of the inconsistent linguistic and syntactic textures found in the *Poruḷatikāram* by working through the problems of organization, the arrangement of stanzas, interpolation, and the influence of Sanskrit. Takahashi divides the *Poruḷatikāram* into four discrete chronological layers, with the earliest dating from the first through the third centuries C.E. and the later, more "Sanskritic," segments from the fourth through the sixth centuries C.E.[17]

The Sanskrit Corpus

Though thought by some to be the work of a single poet, the poems of the Sanskrit *Amaruśataka* probably compose an early anthology, the compilation of which is attributed to Amaru, a legendary king. There are a number of tales about the identity of Amaru. One version is retold by Siegfried Lienhard:

> Thanks to his powers of yoga, the great master of Advaita-vedānta, Śaṅkarācārya, once entered [the dead king Amaru's] body, [made love to his hundred wives] and, by virtue of this trick, was able to answer certain questions on the science of love asked him by the wife of the Mîmāṃsā teacher Mandanamiśra [who had challenged him to a debate].[18]

The *Amaruśataka* ("One Hundred Verses [compiled] by Amaru") is considered by Western scholars and by the Sanskrit tradition itself to be a work of extraordinary literary merit, and is often quoted in famous Sanskrit treatises on literature such as Mammaṭa's twelfth-century *Kāvyaprakaśa* ("A Clarification of Poetry"). I have also chosen a few poems drawn from segments of the *Subhāṣitaratnakoṣa* ("A Treasury of Well-Spoken Verse") in order to widen and enhance the Sanskrit sample. This anthology was probably compiled sometime before 1100 C.E. by Vidyākara, a Buddhist scholar who is said to have worked in the Jagaddala monastery in what is now Malda District in West Bengal. The poems are by various authors whose dates range principally from the eighth to the eleventh centuries C.E. Like those of the *Amaruśataka*, its verses are occasionally found as illustrations in rhetorical works.

The Amaru poems were used primarily in Ānandavardhana's ninth-century *Dhvanyāloka* and in Dhanika's commentary on Dhanañjaya's tenth-century *Daśarūpaka*, as well as in the *Kāvyaprakaśa*. These three particular *śāstras* perhaps best illustrate the nuances of how Sanskrit lyric poems should be written and how they should be understood, which is why they are crucial to this study. They also beautifully display the relationship between "lyric" and "drama," touching on all performative aspects of these poems.

The two commentaries on the *Amaruśataka* that are of primary interest are the "Rasikasañjīvinī" of Arjunavarmadeva (ca. 1200 C.E.) and the "Śṛṅgāradīpikā" of Vemabhūpāla (ca. 1400 C.E.). These commentaries are very illuminating, especially when read in tandem. Not only are they thorough, but Vemabhūpāla is often quite critical of Arjunavarmadeva's interpretations. These criticisms are very instructive in working out a "map," as it were, of changing trends in reading and interpreting Sanskrit poetry in this later period of South

Asian literary history. Both commentators were strongly concerned with the issue of *rasa* ("essence," "character," "mood"). The *rasa* of the *Amaruśataka* is *śṛṅgāra* (best translated by the word "desire"), traditionally divided into the two modes known as *sambhoga* ("union") and *vipralambha* ("separation"). Vemabhūpāla cannot even agree with Arjunavarmadeva on the basic identification of mode for some of the poems, let alone some of the more subtle issues involving interpretive nuance. These commentaries often collapse the traditional *sambhoga* and *vipralambha* distinctions, and both commentators generally come to favor *vipralambha* interpretations.

Prākrit *Gāthās*

The Māhārāṣṭrī Prākrit verses of the *Gāthāsaptaśatī* were composed by a number of authors, but it is impossible to determine definite authorship. Any information we have is based on ascriptions that vary from recension to recension. However, it is traditionally and generally accepted that these verses were collected by one man, Hāla, a king of the Sātavāhana dynasty, who ruled from 20 to 24 C.E. in Pratishthana (modern-day Paithan, located in central Maharashtra). Little is known about Hāla. According to some early commentaries, he composed forty-four of the verses contained in the anthology. The verses are in the form of couplets. A great many are found in rhetorical texts, used as examples of *dhvani* poetry. Loosely, *dhvani* means "poetic resonance." I will describe aspects of this critical category at length below.

The *Gāthāsaptaśatī* is "liminal" in many ways. Its liminality is borne out in the language of the poems themselves, which is made up of an odd mixture of what linguists term "middle Indo-Aryan" and Dravidian words. It also represents a strange poeticization—a kind of linguistic "capturing"—of colloquial idioms and sexual language, the latter largely in the forms of asides and double entendre. Like the Amaru poems, the *gāthās* are quoted in the *Kāvyaprakaśa* and the *Dhvanyāloka*. Bhoja also made extensive use of them as illustrations in his eleventh-century *Sarasvatī kaṇṭhābhāraṇa*, a compendious work on *alaṃkāra*, or rhetorical figure.

The commentaries are where the real issues of reading lie. The *gāthās* usually present contextual enigmas that pose interpretive and cultural questions. The extant commentaries on the *Gāthāsaptaśatī* were written in Sanskrit between the fourteenth (Bhūvanapāla, Vemabhūpāla) and the twentieth centuries (Mathurānāth Śāstrī). One is by Gaṅgādharabhaṭṭa, whose date we do not precisely know, though Paul Dundas places him in the sixteenth century.[19] There is another commentary by Pītāmbara (date unknown) which is distinguished by the technique of interpreting each couplet in terms of the four *puruṣārthas* ("goals of man"; *dharma, artha, kāma,* and *mokṣa*; "righteousness," "wealth," "love," and "liberation"). To turn the erotic into the didactic is a prosaic commentatorial trick. Ravicandra's commentary on the *Amaruśataka,* which is also of this type, presents the *śṛṅgāra* and *mokṣa* arguments for each verse. This technique allows the commentator to acknowledge erotic issues, and then to avoid them entirely. This line of reasoning is still accepted today. In a preface to his English translation of the *Gāthāsaptaśatī*, Radhagovind Basak asserts that these Prākrit couplets were written in order to teach people how *not* to behave. But Gaṅgādhara's commentary on the *gāthās* does not sidestep the eroticism in the poems. In fact, if anything, he has erred in the opposite direction by claiming that every single couplet in the *Gāthāsaptaśatī* has erotic meaning.

Mathurānāth Śāstrī's commentary is the most comprehensive. For each *gāthā,* he has very carefully catalogued most of the preexisting citations from Ānandavardhana, Mammaṭa, and especially Bhoja. He has also included Gaṅgādharabhaṭṭa but has basically dismissed him as a lunatic. At the very end of the exhaustive (and useful) list for each poem, his own interpretation is added.

Commonalities

There are, at least superficially and structurally, some characteristics that all these collections of poetry hold in common. For example, as Miner has written, "It is impossible to find an example of a literate culture without collections, the motives being the desire to preserve and the desire to honor the especially valued."[20] And clearly, anthology making was a Pan-Indian translinguistic phenomenon. It was a courtly activity that was encouraged and commissioned by kings who, evidently, also sometimes participated in the composition and collection of poetry.

Save for the Sanskrit *Subhāṣitaratnakoṣa,* all the anthologies which I have mentioned have commentaries. Only fragments of Old Tamil commentaries on these anthologies have survived, which raises a point addressed by many of the later Tamil commentators in the form of an almost stock phrase. For example, one of the great commentators on the *Tolkāppiyam,* Pērāciriyar (ca. thirteenth century C.E.), says in his remarks on *Marapiyal*[21] that there had been "a time when there were no commentaries, and literary works were easily understood by everyone."[22] By the time of the twelfth-century grammar, *Naṉṉūl,* "a more or less fixed and rather elaborate conception of what an expository book should look like had developed."[23] At the very end of an exhaustive list of everything a book should have, the author of *Naṉṉūl* stated that it must have a commentary or commentaries.

Just as anthology making was commissioned by courts, so was the composition of commentaries. Generally speaking, many of them were written by kings (or, perhaps more likely, by scholars who were attached to courts and wrote under the names of their patrons). It seems that commenting on a text was (and still is) a way of showing that it was highly valued.

Another element common to all the anthologies is that the characters that populate these poems seem to be drawn from a similar stock set for each of the three literatures. There are heroes and heroines, the woman's friend, the man's friend, "other women" (and, less frequently, "other men"), go-betweens, and parents. The Tamil and Prākrit poets also include the heroine's wet nurse or foster mother. The Tamil poets add itinerant musicians and dancers who act as messengers and also have a fully developed sense of how parents fit in with the romantic lives of their children. There are poems of separation in the Tamil anthologies that are spoken by mothers who are pining for their daughters who have eloped, "married down," or are living in a far-off place. These are still classified as "love poems," and are unique to Tamil. An example from *Naṟṟiṇai* follows, poem 110.[24] The speaker is the heroine's mother:

I held in one hand
a pot of glowing gold
full of sweet milk,
white and tasty,
mixed with honey.
I ordered her to eat
and as I beat her,
raising a small rod
with a soft tip
wound round with cloth,
she toddled away,
her golden anklets clattering
with their fresh-water pearls inside.

That little prankster,
who ran under a canopy
so that the good, old nurses,
their hair gray and thinning,
would slow down and stop in their tracks,
where did she learn this knowledge,
these manners?

As her husband's family grows poor,
she doesn't think once
of the rich rice her father used to give
and more pliable
than fine black sand
under running water,
she eats when she can,
that little one
with such great strength.

When read against the background of Sanskrit poetry, the above poem is utterly jarring—the expression of such a sentiment simply does not exist in the Sanskrit erotic tradition, save for in later devotional texts such as the *Bhāgavata-purāṇa,* which is clearly informed by Dravidian aesthetic sensibilities. The girl is fed milk and honey from a golden pot. When she refuses it, she is beaten, although the rod her mother wields is padded with cloth to soften the blows.

For reasons of comparison, I have chosen anthologies or sections of anthologies that are topically similar. They treat the subject of love in all of its various forms. Even from a statistical standpoint, love poetry was the most significant type composed. Love poems overwhelm anthologies that are not even devoted specifically to the topic, and the conventions of this genre were adopted by later devotional traditions. Even more specifically, the topic of love in separation is, statistically speaking, of greater significance. This includes poems composed in the *rasa,* or mood, of *vipralambha-śṛñgāra* in Sanskrit and Prākrit and in the Tamil *tiṇais* of *neytal, marutam,* and *pālai,* which are all related to separation of one kind or another. Out of the 101 verses in Vemabhūpāla's recension of the *Amaruśataka,* for instance, all but twenty-seven are identified as *vipralambha* poems. For Tamil, in all of the *akam* texts in the *cañkam* corpus, out of 1,859 poems, 1,137 have been identified as belonging to the landscapes of separation. *Pālai,* the desert landscape of abject separation, tops the list at 530; *mullai,* the landscape of domestic happiness (and patient, trusting separation) after marriage, is the least popular, with a total of 234 poems.[25]

The question is, why love? And why separation and not the bliss of union, sexual or otherwise? We are all preoccupied with love on one level or another—having it, not having it—for even ascetics are consciously averse to it. In a way, it is the primary human preoccupation and will probably always be the ultimate distraction. But it goes much deeper than this, and at the end of my discussions here, I suggest that perhaps this marked obsession in the realm of literature has to do more with questions of the acuity of human experience in the realms of power and dominance and their curious ties with ambiguity than it has to do with love or lust.

Divergences

At this point, it would be fruitful to have a look at three poems, one each from Sanskrit, Tamil, and Prākrit. All three share one object, a parrot, an identifiable erotic "rhetorical trigger" in all three literatures. Let us chase this object through several centuries of poetry to see what it can tell us about changes and differences in poetics. The first poem is number 616 from the *Subhāṣitaratnakoṣa*. The poem has no ascribed author. The verse forms part of a section titled "The Evidence of Consummation" *(samāptanidhuvanacihnavrajyā)*. The second poem, by Kapilar, is from the *Aiṅkuṟunūṟu*. This verse is one of ten about parrots from a section of the work entitled *Kiḷḷai-p-pattu* ("Ten on Parrots"). The decad is, in turn, a part of a hundred-verse section entirely composed by Kapilar on "love in union," the context of the *kuṟiñci* landscape. The last verse is number 1.75 from the *Gāthāsaptaśatī*. Here are the three poems:

At daybreak,
when the parrot
was bent on mimicking
her cries of passion
in front of her elders,
the doe-eyed girl,
embarrassed,
drowned it out
by jangling
her stacks of bangles,
clapping
as if to make
the children dance in play.

(*Subhāṣitaratnakoṣa* 616)

May parrots outlive
the flood at the end of time!

They've caused this clatter
made by the long arms
of the woman
with the thick black hair
and many gleaming jewels.

(*Aiṅkuṟunūṟu* 281)

Look,

rubies and emeralds mixed
fall from heaven

like a necklace unstrung
from the throat of the sky-goddess:

A line of parrots.

(*Gāthāsaptaśatī* 1.75)

It is clear that all three authors have chosen to use the parrot as a symbol of one sort or another. The Sanskrit verse is an erotic sketch, an almost painterly object; a sexual vignette. In the original Sanskrit, it is also heavily embellished—encrusted with elaborate rhetorical ornamentation—a piece of high Sanskrit rococo. The ornaments are particularly apparent in the onomatopoeia in the long compound word in the second line.[26] Nothing is left to the imagination and all possible elements are incorporated—time, the parrot and the function of the parrot, bedroom moans, judgmental in-laws, the girl, her eyes and her embarrassment, and the noise she makes as she tries to cover up her "crime." Everything is *in praesentia;* the poem moves in a linear fashion and its meaning is syntagmatically conveyed.

The eroticism of the Tamil verse from the *Aiṅkuṟunūṟu* is less apparent. Again, the parrot is a cause. The theme *(tuṟai)* of the verse is called "the guarding of the millet" *(puṉaṅkāval)* in Tamil poetics, identified as such by Cāminātaiyar. The male speaker of the poem is praising the parrots because their raids on the outlying millet fields bring the young women outside. The women rush to the fields with sticks and clappers to frighten off the plundering birds. These fields are places of tryst and the verse implies a happy memory of a certain girl with abundant hair and glittering jewelry. The poem is spare, unlike the Sanskrit verse. Its complexity lies in its semantics. The parrot here is not simply a causal element but a "paradigmatic" one, as well; its presence in the verse alludes to certain erotic paradigms of which it is a part, moving the poem to a third dimension of resonance, fetching a memory of love and inciting a renewed longing.

That the Prākrit poem is an erotic verse may not be at all apparent to a reader who is unfamiliar with the commentarial literature. It strikes us at first as a beautiful descriptive verse: a simile and nothing more. As we will see, this verse is erotic not because of the presence of specifically erotic elements, but because of the absence of these very elements. The eroticism is dependent both on poetic resonance *(dhvani)* and on simple *poetic diction.* Let us assume for a moment that a male speaker is addressing a woman whom he wants to seduce. The parrots' descent from the sky to the trees and downward brings the girl's eye from the sky to the ground. The ground beneath the trees is where trysts take place in Prākrit poems. The unstrung necklace suggests the unraveling of, perhaps, the woman's innocence but may refer to the breaking or the throwing off of a necklace during lovemaking, a theme in other Prākrit poems.

In both the Tamil verse and the *gāthā,* the varying degrees of absence of explicit erotic elements lead the reader toward a certain type of literary participation. The Sanskrit verse asks us to admire it. It is a closed system. Everything in it is domestic as well as domesticated—the parrot is a caged pet, as is the housebound wife, and there is no mention of the world outside. The Tamil poem asks us to praise parrots, to share in a memory, and to help create a collective longing. But the Prākrit verse seduces us right along with the woman to whom it might have been addressed. With its very first word, it commands us to "look" from the sky to the ground and to enter into a sensual (as well as a literary) brand of participation with it. So, the Prākrit *gāthās* have a special, rather uncanny relationship with the world of classical Sanskrit poetics through *dhvani,* "suggestion," or, more explicitly, "poetic resonance."

The above paragraphs have demonstrated one way in which three poets from three distinct traditions have understood and incorporated into their poems an image which is common in their physical and literary environments. To illustrate how commentarial interpretations might differ, let us turn to two commentators, Mathurānāth Śāstrî and Gaṅgādharabhaṭṭa, to see the sort of interpretive choices that commentators might make as they encounter that final Prākrit verse.

Mathurānāth Śāstrī's headnote reads, "A certain man who was strolling in a garden said this to the woman walking next to him in order to incite love in her heart." In the commentary that follows the poem, Mathurānāth Śāstrī addresses the metaphor in the verse in a very direct way, which is actually somewhat rare. He begins with the traditional paraphrase:

> You look at the line of parrots falling from heaven like a necklace (called *kaṇṭhī*); like a necklace composed of (strung with) emerald and ruby stones that has broken from the middle of the sky-goddess' throat. Because of the green color of the parrots, they look like emerald gems, and because of the red color of their beaks, they are the same as rubies. Thus, this verse is a metaphor, and moreover, it is indicated to the beloved woman that this is the time for savoring love.

(It is unclear to me where Mathurānāth Śāstrī gets this last idea.)

Another commentator, Gaṅgādharabhaṭṭa, simply states: "A certain woman who is intent on having sex said this to fix her lover's mind on something else for the sake of making their pleasure last longer." Gaṅgādharabhaṭṭa has provided this interpretation for a very specific set of poems that happens to include this one, and I will discuss it at length below.

In the following pages, I provide analyses via close readings of approximately fifteen poems selected from the anthologies in light of the literary *śāstras* and commentaries that discuss them. The analyses will be preceded by a section which will compare how Tamil and Sanskrit rhetoricians have understood the goal of aesthetic response; that is, how both traditions understand this aspect of the act of "reading." A technical comparison of issues of aesthetic response in the Tamil and Sanskrit traditions will be useful in laying the theoretical groundwork for the later sections which analyze each genre separately.

Aesthetic Response

Analogs do exist in Tamil for the Sanskrit notions of *rasa* and *dhvani*. The author of the *Tolkāppiyam* has called them *mey-p-pāṭu* and *iṟaicci* respectively. Here, I would like to address these issues briefly. Scholars have been too hasty in simply dismissing the Tamil concept of *mey-p-pāṭu* as a straightforward translation of Sanskrit *rasa*. The author of the *Tolkāppiyam* has given it a full chapter, and modern commentators are concerned with identifying what the *mey-p-pāṭu* is for each poem. Zvelebil translates both *rasa* and *mey-p-pāṭu* as "mood." Although he is correct in an overarching sense, this does not at all reflect the technical or rhetorical differences in how these processes come into play during aesthetic response.

The very words themselves indicate lexically that the processes are quite different. The Sanskrit word *rasa* has a wide range of meaning, but the most relevant ones in this case are "juice," "essence," or "flavor." *Rasa* was first used to describe aesthetic experience in Bharata's *Nāṭyaśāstra,* a compendious text on dramatic representation that was composed at around the second century B.C.E. by Bharata.[27] In brief, *rasa* is what is produced by *bhāva* ("emotion") in combination with *abhinaya* ("dramatic gesture").[28] *Rasa* is the distillate of emotion and gesture produced by actors on a stage (or by characters in a poem), and it is this distillate that is savored—experienced—by the *rasika* (the "taster" or connoisseur). There is no *rasa* without a *rasika.*

In contrast, the Tamil notion of *mey-p-pāṭu,* which can best be translated by the phrase "physical manifestation of the emotions," is what happens to the performers on the stage or the characters in a poem as well as to the audience or "reader," as K. Paramasivam suggests.[29] In Sanskrit terms, this represents a collapsing of *rasa* into *bhāva,* which is certainly how most later devotional traditions want to understand *rasa.* The Tamil tradition understands aesthetic experience as a much more direct sort of phenomenon than does the Sanskrit tradition. It is possible that the author of the chapter on *mey-p-pāṭu* in the last section of the *Tolkāppiyam* interpreted the Sanskrit notion of *rasa* in this way, either through a true "misreading" of the *Nāṭyaśāstra* (which may well be six or seven centuries earlier in date than this portion of the *Tolkāppiyam* if we choose to accept Zvelebil's dates) or through a "rereading" or "reworking" of this rather complicated idea.

No one has written much on Tamil aesthetic response. Save for a section of Pērāciriyar's thirteenth-century commentary on this portion of the *Tolkāppiyam,* there is nothing available. Here is a summary of Pērāciriyar's understanding of *mey-p-pāṭu*:

> To one who has tasted neem, there is the sense of bitterness. But the person who watches someone tasting neem does not taste it on his own tongue. He knows with his sight that the other man has tasted something bitter. Like this, if one person sees another person running in terror because he has seen something fearful, the observer need not see the large-toothed lion in order to recognize that the man is afraid.[30]

Unfortunately, there is an ambiguity in the text that can lead us to two different conclusions. The first is that the audience will identify with the performer or character and will feel what he is feeling. The second is that the fear or sense of bitterness is recognized intellectually by the audience but not necessarily felt. The audience might feel compassion or amusement instead. One of the problems with the extract cited from Pērāciriyar's commentary is that he is responding to an earlier commentator with whom he disagrees. The earlier commentator's work, unfortunately, has long been lost. Paramasivam has suggested that this earlier argument must have been in support of the notion that the audience directly feels what the actor is feeling—if the actor laughs or cries, so does the audience.[31]

Just as scholars tend to equate *mey-p-pāṭu* with *rasa,* so do they equate Tamil *iṟaicci* with Sanskrit *dhvani,* when, again, the processes are quite different. Lexically, *dhvani* means "sound," "reverberation," "resonance." The root meaning of *iṟaicci* is "flesh." By extension, in poetics it refers to the suggestive meaning conveyed by the *karu-p-poruḷs* (the physical elements—flora and fauna—that grow and flourish inside each of the five landscapes in the Tamil system). These techniques are achieved in quite different ways. Readers must know these semiotic systems in order to be able to understand the poems in their respective languages, since both systems contain elaborate poetic codings of word and gesture that require a certain amount of sophistication and education.

Dhvani is a term that refers to many areas of poetic application. It can allude to the bell of recognition that is struck in one's head upon understanding a pun or a double-entendre, and this is actually how most of the commentators choose to use the term. For the sake of illustration, let us consider the following Prākrit *gāthā:*

Her husband,
given to jealousy,
won't let her gather
honey flowers
at night,

but Mother,
that simpleton

will go and do it
all by himself.

(*Gāthāsaptaśatī* 2.59)

The meaning of this poem is fairly opaque without the contexts provided by the commentators. Mathurānāth Śāstrī's headnote and commentary help us to understand the various levels of *dhvani* in this little poem. The headnote reads: "A messenger said this, under the guise of chatting with a neighbor woman, in order to indicate to her friend's lover a different trysting place, which was previously established to be a thicket of honey flowers." The commentary begins with the usual paraphrase. Then, in sum, it reads:

> Because he doesn't know about her tryst with her lover which is going on in his house, his nature is simple. Moreover, it is suggested to the lover (who is probably within earshot): "You shouldn't go to the honey-flower thicket; rather, go to her very house without fear." What is indicated by the word *eva* in the phrase *svayam eva,* "all by himself," is this: because there is no help in gathering the honey flower blossoms from another person, he won't come back to the house quickly. Therefore, a state of safety, as well, is suggested to the woman's lover.

Let us compare this with a Tamil poem, *Kuṟuntokai* 272,[32] that contains *iṟaicci,* achieved through a technique called *uḷḷuṟai-y-uvamam,* "comparison by means of a hidden meaning." This poem is spoken by a man who, according to U. Vē. Cāminātaiyar's headnote, has been ridiculed by his companion.

What he said:

I wonder
if I'll ever touch her again.
    Her elder brothers have fine bows
    and they whistle and toss stones
    to flush an innocent, sad-eyed doe
    from her cover and separate her
    from her herd in the wide-spaced forest.

    She stands before them
    as they plunge red-shafted arrows

into the breast
of her raging, swift buck
and rip them out with blood.

That girl from the hills,
her hair dark and fragrant,
has black-rimmed eyes
shaped like those arrowheads,
points placed opposite each other
and I wonder
if I will ever again touch
those shoulders of hers.

The Prākrit poem exudes an elusive, polysemic *dhvani,* but the Tamil poem has a set and unwavering code bordering on allegory that the reader must understand in order to appreciate the verse fully. We know from the *kuṟiñci* context that the speaker and his lover have already met and have had intercourse. He encounters her brothers in the woods and watches them as they flush a doe from her hiding place with the intention of drawing out the male behind her. The doe stands watching as the brothers kill the buck. The speaker is afraid of the woman's brothers and of what they will do to him if their love is found out. He gives voice to this fear by referring to his lover as the doe and himself as the stag. Her eyes are also shaped like the arrow flints, and pierce his heart just as the arrows pierce the heart of the stag. This particular poem is not so difficult to decipher once the reader is aware of the system, which is based on the *karu-p-poruḷs* of its particular landscape.

It can be seen in the preceding paragraphs that although literary conventions in the three traditions are similar to a certain extent, techniques of reading differ greatly, depending largely on precisely what a reader has to know to decode specific symbolic paradigms in order to make sense out of a poem. In the following section, these techniques will be articulated, elaborated upon, and compared in depth.

2

Reading "North" and "South": Issues of Comparative Reading and the Classical Poetry of South Asia

I have already alluded to some major differences in the ways in which Tamil, Sanskrit, and Prākrit love poems have been read and understood by "competent" readers, that is, by readers of poetry who have "internalized the grammar of literature," permitting them to "convert linguistic sequences into literary structures and meanings."[1] In the next few pages, I will delineate in far greater detail some of the more fundamental differences in various reading processes in these three literary traditions. Specifically, I will compare what I identified above as the three most important critical notions of these genres, namely, *tiṇai*, *rasa*, and *dhvani*. The comparisons will be based on what readers have to know when they read classical poems and on how they should ideally process information in poetry. I will begin with brief summaries and comparisons of some of the most basic principles of Sanskrit and Tamil poetics. These comparisons will cast into high relief some fundamental differences in the elements crucial to the composition and interpretation of classical poems.

Rasa

The ninth-century Kashmiri critic Ānandavardhana, one of the greatest of all Sanskrit rhetoricians, identified *rasa* as the goal of poetry, with *dhvani* as its means.[2] Śaṅkuka, a commentator on the *Nāṭyaśāstra,* who may have been Ānandavardhana's contemporary, defined *rasa* as an actor's imitation of the *bhāva*—the "emotion" or "state of being in mind or in body"—that theoretically exists in the fictive character being portrayed, and as something for the delight of the audience.[3] The *Nāṭyaśāstra* has provided us with a standard list of eight possible *rasas*: the erotic *(śṛṅgāra),* the comic *(hāsya),* the compassionate *(karuṇa),* the cruel *(raudra),* the valorous *(vīra),* the terrible *(bhayānaka),* the abhorrent *(bībhatsā),* and the miraculous *(adbhuta).*[4] Each *rasa* is based on the aesthetic transformation of an underlying human emotion termed a *sthāyibhāva* (literally, a "permanent feeling"). In the following columns the eight *rasas* are listed with their corresponding *sthāyibhāvas:*

Rasa	Corresponding *sthāyibhāvas*
erotic *(śṛṅgāra)*	passion *(rati)*
comic *(hāsya)*	mirth *(hāsa)*
compassionate *(karuṇa)*	grief *(śoka)*
cruel *(raudra)*	anger *(krodha)*
valorous *(vīra)*	exertion *(utsāha)*
terrible *(bhayānaka)*	fear *(bhaya)*
abhorrent *(bībhatsā)*	disgust *(jugupsā)*
miraculous *(adbhuta)*	astonishment *(vismaya)*

underlying human emotion

The relationship between each *rasa* and its *sthāyibhāva* can be easily explained if we examine the pairing of the comic, *hāsya,* with mirth, or *hāsa.* The literal and most basic root meaning of the word *hāsya* (which is, technically speaking, a gerundive) is "to be laughed at," that is, comical or ridiculous. *Hāsa* is a noun meaning "laughter" or "mirth." From this, we can see that the list of *sthāyibhāvas* is composed of nouns describing human emotions and that each corresponding *rasa* is—for many theoreticians—what an audience is expected to experience. Although the other seven pairings in the list do not have the same kind of grammatical relationship as *hāsya* and *hāsa,* the conceptual relationship between each pair is the same.

Therefore, *rati* is passion and *śṛṅgāra* is the aesthetic experience of desire evoked by a portrayal of passion; *śoka* is grief and *karuṇa* is the aesthetic experience of compassion evoked by a portrayal of grief, and so on.

The system is further articulated by elements that, according to *Nāṭyaśāstra* 6.31, actually produce *rasa:* "*Rasa* is effected from the combination of *vibhāvas, anubhāvas,* and *vyabhicāribhāvas.*"[5] First are the *vibhāvas* ("causes," "determinants"), which were later divided into two categories, the *ālambanavibhāvas* (literally, "the determinants which are supports," or "objective determinants") and the *uddīpanavibhāvas* ("the determinants that are excitants," or "stimulative determinants").[6] Second are the *anubhāvas,* the "after-feelings," the indications of feelings through gestures, "consequents." Third are the thirty-three *vyabhicāribhāvas,* the "transitory feelings," the transitional states of mind or body.

In his introduction to his translation of the *Dhvanyāloka,* Daniel H.H. Ingalls explains the ways in which these elements interact to produce *rasa:*

> The objective determinants *(ālambanavibhāvas)* are the objects toward which the emotions are felt. In the erotic flavor they will be the lover and his beloved. . . . The stimulative determinants *(uddīpanavibhāvas)* . . . will be such factors as the springtime, gardens, or a bridal chamber. . . . The consequents of the emotions may be regarded by the audience as its symptoms; in the erotic flavor, for example, they will include the sidelong glances, smiles, [and] graceful movements of the limbs.[7]

Added to this list are eight *sāttvikabhāvas,* "involuntary" or "true" bodily states. These are the eight physical states that are caused by natural emotion. They are paralysis *(stambha),* perspiration *(sveda),* gooseflesh *(romañca),* stammering *(svaravikāra* or *svarabheda),* trembling *(vepathu),* change in color *(varṇavikāra* or *vaivarṇya),* tears *(aśru),* and fainting *(pralaya).*[8]

The evocation of *śṛṅgārarasa* is the goal of Sanskrit love poetry. The prose section following *Nāṭyaśāstra* 6.45 recognizes two loci *(adhiṣṭhānas)* for the depiction of *śṛṅgārarasa.* They are love in union *(sambhoga)* and love in separation *(vipralambha)*. The following two poems from the *Amaruśataka* will illustrate the two loci. According to the headnotes of the commentator Arjunavarmadeva,[9] both poems are spoken by a woman to her entourage of girlfriends. The second poem in this set is a particularly nice example of a *vipralambha* verse because it employs a number of *anubhāvas* prescribed by the *Nāṭyaśāstra* for the portrayal of this locus. These *anubhāvas* also correspond to several items on the list of the ten symptoms of lovesickness described in Vatsyāyana's *Kāmasūtra*, verse 5.1.5.[10]

A woman said this when asked by her girlfriends, "How was your lover in bed?"

When my lover came to bed,
the knot came untied
all by itself.

My dress,
held up by the strings of a loosened belt,
barely stayed on my hips.

Friend,
that's as much as I know now.

When he touched my body,
I couldn't at all remember
who he was,
who I was,
or how It was.

(*Amaruśataka* 101, *sambhoga*)

A certain woman, weary of her girlfriends' insistence that she should display jealous anger, scolded them:

Sighs parch my mouth.
My heart's torn out by the roots.
Sleep won't come.
I can't see my lover's face.
Day and night I cry
and my limbs have withered,

ever since I ignored my lover
who had fallen at my feet.

Friends,
what good were you counting on
when you made me be angry
at that dear man?

(*Amaruśataka* 92, *vipralambha*)

These two poems make it obvious that their author(s) were highly conscious of the different elements that are needed to produce *rasa*. At first glance, it seems that the first poem hardly requires an explanation, only that the forgetting of the details of lovemaking or "playing dumb" is a fairly common way of bypassing graphic description (something that the tradition eschews, although there are certainly exceptions), while at the same time saying that the lovemaking was good. However, when the technicalities of the evocation of *rasa* are taken into account, it becomes obvious that the poet has skillfully manipulated these very injunctions against "graphic description" and has, in fact, assimilated them into a very effective trope. The charm of this verse is generated by the woman's inability to satisfy her girlfriends with an elaborate description of physical details. The reader, right along with the audience of girlfriends, is tantalized by the woman's slow description not of what was done but of what the woman could and (more crucially) could not remember.

The second poem, with its list of classic symptoms and complaints, lets the reader know that the woman is still in love with the man. She is searching for other ways to win him over. There is a tension in *vipralambha* poems that uninitiated readers often miss. We can be absolutely assured that the woman will be reunited with her lover or that a strong possibility of a reunion exists. Otherwise, the poem would evoke another *rasa* such as *karuṇa* (compassion), something that Sanskrit critics do not allow in poems of this type.

Rasa is something tasted or experienced, not felt. Ingalls has explained this beautifully: "*Rasa* is not simply the apprehension of another person's mental state. It is rather a supernormal relishing based on an involved sympathy."[11] Ingalls is describing an important aesthetic distinction that can be understood through the act of comparing Sanskrit textual prescriptions with similar concerns in Tamil texts for the ways in which poetry should properly be appreciated. A "distancing" (Ingalls's "supernormal relishing") should ideally occur between what is represented by a text and its appreciator. In contrast, the Tamil tradition does not seem to acknowledge "distancing" as a requirement for proper aesthetic appreciation.

Rasa and the *Meyppāṭṭiyal*

When we turn to the sixth chapter of the Tamil *Poruḷatikāram,* the *Meyppāṭṭiyal,* we encounter an obvious attempt "to incorporate the Sanskritic *bhāvas/rasas* into Tamil poetics."[12] The third verse of this chapter lists eight *mey-p-pāṭus* ("conditions of the body")[13] that roughly correspond to the eight Sanskrit *rasas.* They are laughter *(nakai),* weeping *(aḻukai),* disgust *(iḷivaral),* awe *(maruṭkai),* fear *(accam),* heroism *(perumitam),* anger *(vekuḷi),* and delight *(uvakai).* Verse 204 of the *Ceyyuḷiyal*[14] defines *mey-p-pāṭu* in this way: "That which will effect a physiological reaction by means of a clearly stated predominant theme is *mey-p-pāṭu.*"[15] It is apparent that the list is intended to be the same as the list of Sanskrit *rasas,* but the author of this *iyal* has reordered them and has obviously understood them differently. *Perumitam,* homologous to Sanskrit *vīra,* "heroism," is really the only item on the Tamil list that would be considered a true *rasa* by a Sanskrit rhetorician. *Aḻukai,* "weeping," which is probably meant to be analogous to *karuṇa,* "compassion," would be classified as a *sāttvikabhāva* in the Sanskrit system, and the remaining six items on the list would fall under the category of *bhāva.* Other scholars have suggested that the *Meyppāṭṭiyal* must have been a later addition to the *Tolkāppiyam,*[16] as it is an obvious borrowing from Sanskrit dramaturgical theory.

The differences in just how *rasa* was "read" by the author(s) of the *Tolkāppiyam* have been consistently glossed over by scholars except for Norman Cutler, who has pointed out that "Tamil poeticians seemed to be unaware of the essential difference between *bhā va* and *rasa.* . . . Tamil poetics does not explicitly acknowledge the difference between character and event in the purely literary context and in the "real" world inhabited by the audience, though this distinction is axiomatic to the poetics of *rasa*."[17]

The two major and most widely accepted English translations of the *Tolkāppiyam* can give us a clue to the extent to which *rasa* has long been differently interpreted by the Tamil literary establishment. For example, Ilakkuvanar's translation[18] of the verse in the *Ceyyuḷiyal* that defines *mey-p-pāṭu* reads, "*Mey-p-pāṭu* is to make the composition so easy and simple as to make *the reader*[19] exhibit his psychic feelings by physical changes on reading or hearing it." Likewise, P. S. Subrahmanya Sastri's translation[20] of the same verse reads: "If the description of an object is so vivid that one can enjoy it with hair bristling, eyes shedding tears, etc., it is called *mey-p-pāṭu*." However, we must bear in mind that there is absolutely nothing in the verse in the original Tamil text or in either medieval commentary that mentions a site for the occurrence of *mey-p-pāṭu:* there is no mention of reader, audience, or actor.

It is clear that these two systems are vastly different in the ways in which they describe the reconstitution of reality in drama and poetry, and they are also very different in the ways in which these "reconstitutions" are received by audiences and readers. Ingalls has described the perception of *rasa* by a Sanskrit audience as "sympathetic." It might also be described as indirect and intellectualized, as a somewhat diverted emotional heightening produced somewhere between text and reader. A Tamil reader's response to a poem has been traditionally understood as empathetic and direct; it is also interesting to note here that, while the Sanskrit rhetoricians were very concerned about connoisseurship, there is nothing in the *Tolkāppiyam* or in any other Tamil text on rhetoric that explicitly mentions it.

The author(s) of the *Tolkāppiyam* and subsequent commentators on it and on the *cañkam* anthologies thought that *mey-p-pāṭu* was an important concept, but certainly not a central one. One gets the sense that responding to a poem or to a dramatic work was a "given," and that aesthetic response was something that did not require much mental reflection or intellectual articulation. It definitely did not require a "supernormal relishing" or, to put it more precisely, the "feeling of a feeling." Rather than *mey-p-pāṭu,* the concept that is central to the understanding of classical Tamil poetry is *tiṇai,* and I now wish to shift my discussion to this concept, which is the hallmark of Tamil poetics. Just as *rasa* had become the primary focus of the Sanskrit rhetoricians and commentators, so had *tiṇai* become the chief concern of the Tamil critics.

Tiṇai

Tiṇai is an extremely difficult word to translate neatly. The word "landscape" and the phrase "poetic situation" are currently the accepted and the most widely used definitions, but there is a problem with both. The problem is one of scope and boundary. *Tiṇai* is, in a very real sense, the artistic space circumscribed by the poets, along with everything contained therein. I tentatively choose the word "context" to translate *tiṇai,* but what must be understood is that this context includes geographical space, time, and everything that grows, develops, and lives within that space and time, including emotion. The *Tolkāppiyam* stresses that emotion (or mood) is the only thing within a *tiṇai* that is actually fixed, a rather difficult concept to grasp but crucial to the understanding of this system.[21] I would like to turn now to the *Tolkāppiyam* itself and examine the way in which the system of Tamil poetics is literally built "from the ground up."

The first *iyal* of the *Poruḷatikāram* is the *Akattiṇaiyiyal,* "The Chapter on Interior Contexts," describing the requirements for *akam* poetry, poems about one's "inner life." The first few verses of this chapter give the basis and set all limits for spatial dimensions and orientations, as well as corresponding fourth-dimensional aspects of time and season:

1. It is said that there are seven contexts which have been mentioned previously, beginning with *kaikkiḷai* (the context of "minor relationship," or one-sided love) and ending with *peruntiṇai* (ironically, the "major context"; that of mismatched love).

2. The middle five contexts, save for the middlemost (which is *pālai* in the traditional list, the context set in the desert), have the quality of being divided into lands attached to sounding waves.
3. When investigating poetic practices, these three are obvious in the following order: *mutaṟporuḷ*—the "primal" or "first" elements, those of space and time; *karupporuḷ* or "germinal elements"—"regional features," the features that germinate and grow inside space and time as circumscribed by the *mutaṟporuḷ*; and the *uripporuḷ*, or "behavioral elements," those of mood, emotion, and so on.

In this discussion, I will only be concerned with the "middle five contexts," for which the author of the *Tolkāppiyam* goes on to assign gods, types of people and their occupations, drums, plants, birds, and so on, to each region. Below is a list of the regions and the *uripporuḷ*, or "mood," that is associated with each one:

	Region	Mood
1.	*kuṟiñci*	*puṇartal*, "lovers' union"
2.	*mullai*	*iruttal*, "patient waiting for the lover's return"
3.	*pālai*	*piratal*, "separation"
4.	*neytal*	*irañkal*, "lamenting the lover's absence"
5.	*marutam*	*ūṭal*, "jealous quarreling"

Each context is named after a characteristic flower or plant that grows in the tract of land associated with each one. *Pālai* also more generally means desert, and although things do grow there inside the poems, they are generally scrubby, thorny plants, while the other contexts are rife with blooming, fragrant things such as jasmine and blue water lilies. A desert can happen anywhere, and it is significant that it is placed in the middle of the list. This middle placement gives it a central focus, as well as a kind of permeating aspect—it touches all the other contexts, making none of them safe from its desiccating, uncomfortable features. The primary shrubs of *pālai* are evergreen succulents, quite common to all of Tamilnadu even today, while the *kuṟiñci* flower is extremely rare. It grows only in cool mountain tracts and blooms only once in twelve years. The season assigned to *kuṟiñci* is autumn, and its assigned time is midnight; its land tracts are hills and mountains. Associations, therefore, are with rarity, comfort, and coolness, while the *pālai* context is both common and devoid of water. It has summer as its assigned season; high noon is its time.

If we take all of the above into account, the entire *tiṇai* scheme can be thought of as a system of physical/psychic "gestures." This gesturing, however, is not restricted to the human characters in the poems. At times, it seems that the overriding, constant emotional elements (the *uripporuḷs*) associated with each poetic context are actually responsible for animating everything within that context. Feelings belong not only to humans but are also transferred to the physical contexts of which they are a part. The very land itself is capable of showing signs of emotion, as are animals and birds. The following two poems illustrate this beautifully. The first poem is from the *cañkam* anthology *Naṟṟiṇai* and is ascribed to Nallantuvaṉār; the second is from *Kuṟuntokai* and is ascribed to Iḷampūtaṉār.

What her girlfriend said:

Why are you confused
over old deeds we have done?

Live long, Friend,
and don't be sad.
We'll go.
We'll tell him,
and come back.
So get up
and look here.

Like that nectar from the sea
with its rows of waves,
the salt that faces rain,
I fear that you'll melt
and dissolve away.

Facing their man's cruelty to us,
their love for us is great

and they just can't bear it.
Friend,
those fruit-shedding hills of his
will weep waterfalls
of tears.

(*Naṟṟiṇai* 88)

What her girlfriend said, quoting the heroine to make the hero understand her plight:

That man from the shores
with their spreading waters

where a big flock
of small white red-mouthed crows
stays in a grove thick with flowers,
hating the cold
when a spray
cast up by waves
soaks their wet backs
to the skin:

If he leaves me,
my friend,
is there anything
that we will lose,
other than my own sweet life?

(*Kuṟuntokai* 334)

Although the first poem initially appears to be composed on the theme of separation, it is classified as a *kuṟiñci* verse by the modern commentator A. Nārāyaṇācami Aiyar.[22] This is yet another example of a *kuṟiñci* situation in which the initial sexual encounter has already taken place. The heroine is despondent, and her girlfriend speaks words of encouragement to her. The author has artfully manipulated the conventions of one of the landscapes of separation, *neytal,* to express the girlfriend's concern over the heroine's lovesickness. *Neytal,* the landscape of lamentation, builds its poetic language with seaside elements. Here, the girlfriend regards the heroine as a pile of salt left out in the rain to dissolve. As the poem ends, the girlfriend does not appeal to the man himself for mercy but to his land, the fertile, wet, hilly *kuṟiñci* tract, leaving the reader quite literally "in the right place" for the proper understanding of this poem.

The second example is a perfect illustration of a proper *neytal* poem. Cāminātaiyar's headnote infers an even wider gulf of separation between the hero and heroine than the actual poem itself might suggest. The poem is in the heroine's voice, but the girlfriend is actually repeating her very words to the hero to relate to him the heroine's pain and desperation. The initial line of the poem places the reader in the correct frame of reference, as it immediately identifies the man as a *neytal* hero. The poem then describes the heroine's discomfort by means of *uḷḷuṟai-y-uvamam* by invoking the *kaṟupporuḷs* of the *neytal* landscape: the cold, the spray; isolation in a marshy, seaside grove.[23]

Issues of Comparative Reading

One reasonable strategy for formulating a comparison of the two quoted Sanskrit poems with the two Tamil poems above is to categorize *sambhoga-śṛṅgāra-rasa* with *kuṟiñci* and *vipralambha-śṛṅgāra-rasa* with *neytal* (and, by extension, the other three *tiṇais* that encompass situations of separation). It is an understandable reflex to do so; after all, these themes are at least roughly congruent, if not analogous. Although the same themes exist in both traditions, the poems above should make apparent the fact that the two traditions have come to understand these themes differently. For example, it can be surmised that a Sanskrit critic would most likely interpret *Naṟṟiṇai* 88 as a poem about separation rather than one about union, as Nārāyaṇacāmi Aiyar has chosen to do.

For the sake of illustration, let us consider the following two examples, *Aiṅkuṟunūṟu* 210 (attributed to Kapilar) and *Amaruśataka* 99:

> Mother, live long and listen:
>
> When she climbs the dense,
> flesh-smeared stone in our garden
> and stands gazing
> at the flower-covered hills of his land,

her flashing blue jewels will stay put
and we'll find a cure for her stubborn illness.

(*Aiṅkuṟunūṟu* 210)

He is separated from his love
by entire lands,
by hundreds of rivers and mountains,
and by forests
and even if he tries,
he can't stretch his sight that far.

Even though he knows this,
the traveler stretches his neck,
stands on tiptoe,
rubs at his tear-filled eyes,
and, brooding on something,
he looks again
in the direction of his desire.

(*Amaruśataka* 99)

Although at first glance these two poems are strikingly similar in tone, they have in fact been categorized differently by their interpreters. The scenarios are more or less the same. The Tamil poem is spoken by the heroine's friend to the heroine's mother or foster mother and tells of the girl's lovesickness, her "stubborn illness," hinting that the cause of it may lie in the hills overlooking their yard. The hero of the Sanskrit poem is also separated from his lover by a great distance and seeks to cure his sorrow by gazing in her general direction. Although the Sanskrit example is categorized by both major commentators on the *Amaruśataka* as a *vipralambha* poem, the Tamil poem is classified by its author, Kapilar, as a *kuṟiñci* verse, one that depicts lovers' union, even though the lovers are, clearly, physically separated. Once again, if a Sanskrit reader were confronted with this Tamil poem, it would certainly be classified as one evoking *vipralambha*. We only know that the Tamil poem is about lovers' union because of its one synecdochic referent; *avar nāṭṭu-p-pū-k-keḻu kuṉṉu,* "the flower-covered hills of his land." This is the element that identifies the man as a *kuṟiñci* hero, meaning that the reader is to understand that the two have met and have had intercourse. But how does this differentiate the Tamil poem from the Sanskrit one?

This difference in categorization appears to revolve around issues of temporality. *Kuṟiñci* poems appear to incorporate the "love act" with its aftermath, lovesickness; these poems are about "falling in love" or "being in love," as opposed to love that has undergone some sort of legitimization or maturation. In fact, the *Tolkāppiyam* understands the four poetic themes of "separation" as possible only after the relationship between the hero and heroine undergoes just such a process of post-*kuṟiñci* legitimization, either through marriage or through some sort of publicly acknowledged domestic situation that allows love to overripen and go bad. Interestingly enough, elopement is classified as separation—though the lovers are together, they are apart from their families and reliable, familiar creature comforts.

The two chapters following the schematization of *akam* and *puṟam* in the *Poruḷatikāram* are concerned with listing situations that occur during love that is either *kaḷavu* ("stolen," "clandestine") or *kaṟpu* ("chaste"). *Kuṟiñci* poems are always about clandestine love affairs, encompassing all love experiences that have been consummated but before a publicly sanctioned marriage has taken place (secret marriages are allowed in this context). Though the *tiṇais* of *mullai*, *neytal*, and *pālai* can theoretically depict events that occur either before or after a legitimate marriage,[24] statistically speaking, it seems that there is a marriage involved somewhere in the picture that is being destabilized or undermined by the hero's absence or by the introduction of another woman. Moreover, *Kaḷaviyal* 141 explicitly states that a man cannot separate for the purposes of obtaining an education, waging war, or acting as an envoy unless he has been married.

There are, then, really three discernible phases of love in Tamil poetry: falling in love/lovesickness *(kuṟiñci)*, "legitimized" love coupled with increasing degrees of anxiety and tension *(mullai, neytal,* and *marutam)*, and abject or even absolute separation *(pālai)*. Unlike the rhetorical prescriptions prohibiting absolute separation in Sanskrit *śṛṅgāra* poetry (see above), the *Tolkāppiyam* allows it. *Akattiṇaiyiyal* 11 states: "When it appears that . . . separation is permanent, scholars say that the appropriate *tiṇai* is *pālai*."

The Sanskrit critics and poets draw their circles around love experiences in a very different way. As previously stated, there are two major loci considered appropriate for evoking *śṛṅgāra-rasa—sambhoga* and *vipralambha*. The tenth-century author Dhanañjaya[25] has sensitively described three categories in the fourth book of his *Daśarūpa*. In *sūtra* 4.58, Dhanañjaya lists *ayoga, viprayoga,* and *sambhoga* as the three types. *Ayoga* encompasses lovesickness, whereas *viprayoga* is defined as separation between two persons who have a previously established intimate relationship. But, as George Haas explains in his notes to this particular *sūtra, ayoga,* and *viprayoga* "correspond to the *vipralambha* of other treatises,"[26] thereby highlighting a major difference in Sanskrit and Tamil poetic interpretations of these experiences. The "privations," as Haas translates it, of *ayoga* would be categorized as part of the *kuṟiñci* experience—as a facet of union—by Tamil writers, but as an aspect of separation by the Sanskrit establishment.

To think of *vipralambha* as "separation" at all may be a mistake in understanding and/or translation. As Ingalls rightly points out in a note to *Dhvanyaloka* 2.12, "*vipralambhaśṛṅgāra* [is] love in frustration, for *vipralambha* means literally *vañcanā,* deception, frustration."[27] The range of the word's lexical possibilities also underscores the fact that the probability of reunion must necessarily be a part of the mood: *vipralambha* means deception, deceit, and sexual infidelity; it can also theoretically mean reappropriation and recovery. It is this flux in meaning that gives *vipralambha* its added charge; its ambiguity is what can be held responsible for the poetic tension that has served to make this genre so appealing and popular.

The more important differences in reading and interpretive techniques in the Sanskrit and Tamil literary traditions that specifically concern love poetry are, thus, nearly opposite intellectual processes. The extant Sanskrit literary *śāstras* that are concerned with aesthetic response, or "reading," are all ultimately based on the *Nāṭyaśāstra,* a work on drama concerned with all aspects of portrayal, representation, and proper audience response. The classical rhetoricians never escaped its influence. The understanding of a Sanskrit poem is a highly articulated process, and, even though the very basis of much Sanskrit criticism lies in eight (or nine) separate categories of the human emotional experience, direct empathic response is rather routinely condemned by the *śāstras*. Paradoxically, proper connoisseurs must keep their emotions at bay and, instead, must attune their appreciation—their aesthetic response—to the experiencing of *rasa*. It appears that Sanskrit readers are expected to be able to comprehend the significance of a poem through the gestures and natures of its characters, the settings, the "props," and so on: "reading" a Sanskrit poem is like "watching" a Sanskrit play in miniature. Proper appreciation requires a certain amount of emotional disengagement; impressions are ideally assigned to an exterior realm so that even the potential experiencing of the worst sort of despair is transformed into something for aesthetic relish.

In contrast, it seems that engagement and direct empathic response are required of Tamil readers, as well as an ability to internalize a poetics that is based not on emotion but on environment and the ability to attach significance to objects in the poems, decoding them, at times, in ways that smack of the unraveling of an extended allegory. Critic Georges Poulet has written that "the advantage of literature is that it frees one from the usual sense of incompatibility between consciousness and the objects of consciousness."[28] Sanskrit aesthetic theory appears to be based on an urge to maintain this sense of incompatibility on the emotional level, but it is the very erasure of it that is the chief concern and ideal ultimate goal of Tamil poetics. Poulet writes of poetic language and the creation of an "interior universe" in which "external objects are replaced with a congeries of mental objects in close rapport with one's own consciousness."[29] The Tamil *cañkam* writers were obviously never quite free of that sense of incompatibility in their readings of reality: Tamil poetics developed from an acute and inescapable awareness of the incompatibility of the human body and its psychic trappings with the environment in which it moves, lives, and breathes.

The language of the *cañkam* poets arose from a desire for an erasure of the split between self and *tiṇai;* this desire was foisted outward onto the environment, which was then reshaped, literally "incorporated," and made part of their language. In a sense, Tamil poetics is structured very much like Lacan's model of the unconscious.[30] Instead of being an internal and private symbology, it is, in fact, outside, existing in relationships between characters and objects and in what exists between poets and their environments.

Tamil and Sanskrit methods of reading poetry are alike in that there appears to be a notion in both of what constitutes the "proper reading" of a work. Both methods basically assume the notion of an "ideal" reader; the Sanskrit establishment much more explicitly so than the Tamil. One must be a *rasika*, a "taster," or *sahṛdaya*, "like-hearted," in order to appreciate a text properly. As I have stated, though there is no mention of connoisseurship per se in the *Tolkāppiyam*, the author(s) of the text often appeal to anonymous literary authority when setting out basic ideas in its verses: many of them end with the phrase *eṉmaṉār pulavar*, "[so] say the poets."

In other words, a reader must know the conventions in operation, and it can be said that Sanskrit *rasa* theory and the entire system of *tiṇai* in Tamil have enjoyed a long history of employment in the reading of texts (and continue to do so to this day), due to the fact that certain poetic conventions were established at a very early time. The long-standing acceptance of these conventions has led to a pleasant stability in criticism and commentary, but when we turn to the reading and interpretation of Māhārāṣṭrī Prākrit verse, the very idea of "reader competency" and the "proper understanding" of poetry is more or less undone.

It is quite clear that many Prākrit *gāthās* were composed with elements drawn from the same pool of conventions as Sanskrit verse and were manipulated in similar ways, as the following verse illustrates:

She shut her eyes
and imagined her lover on the bed;

hugged herself tight
with her own loose-bangled arms.

(*Gāthāsaptaśatī* 2.33)

A Sanskrit reader would automatically know that this verse describes the agonies of a woman separated from her lover. She is so emaciated from her lovesickness that her bangles no longer fit her properly. But there is also a playful manipulation of the convention, as in the following verse spoken by a guileless heroine:

Friend, tell us.
We ask you
with good feeling:

Why do the bangles
on the wrists
of every woman
grow larger
when their lovers
leave home?

(*Gāthāsaptaśatī* 5.53)

The above two examples only hint at the layers of complexity in the Prākrit genre. Ānandavardhana certainly recognized this complexity, and, as Ingalls has pointed out, his conceptualization of *dhvani* may well have been stimulated by the puzzles presented by Māhārāṣṭrī couplets, as they were composed in a very brief poetic form and could not attain a powerful effect by means other than *dhvani*.[31]

Dhvani

Dhvani means "sound," "echo," "reverberation." Ānandavardhana was clearly indebted to earlier grammarians, especially Bhartṛhari, who first espoused *sphoṭa* theory, which describes the "bursting" of meaning upon the hearing of an utterance. It was upon this that Ānandavardhana based his *dhvani* theory of meaning.[32] Unlike his predecessors, Ānandavardhana was interested only in the aesthetic value of words within the poetic context. *Dhvani* theory describes the significative range of a word or an utterance, and Ānandavardhana understood it as something a step beyond both literal and metaphorical meaning. *Dhvani* theory is a system of meaning in which the signifier is fixed, but its corresponding signifieds are theoretically infinite. Included in the resonant potential of an utterance is its lexicality, that is, its full lexical range, and its associative elements, those things that cannot be expressed by mere lexicality. Additionally, these elements encompass the associations a reader may have with an utterance (that sometimes seem to border on synesthesia), and can even include its opposite meaning.

Let us briefly consider the following example:

Why are you crying
with your head bent down
as the rice fields turn white?

The hemp field's like a dancer,
face daubed with yellow paint.

(*Gāthāsaptaśatī* 1.9)

Commentator Mathurānāth Śāstrī has supplied the following headnote: "There was a meeting place, a rice field, which was frequented by a certain woman in the company of some man. Then, when the rice ripened, seeing that the spot was ruined, a girlfriend informed the crying woman that another meeting spot was available."

The idea is that the rice is ready to be harvested, and if the field is cut, the cover for the woman's amorous meetings is gone. The girlfriend is indicating to her that the hemp field is now a suitable spot for romantic meetings with her lover. The above headnote, actually a paraphrase of the one written by commentator Gaṅgādharabhaṭṭa some four centuries earlier, is not at all enough for Mathurānāth Śāstrī, who claimed to show in his commentary that every single word of the *Gāthāsaptaśatī* contains the potential for *dhvani*.[33] The commentary explains the simile, then suggests other possible levels of meaning, again paraphrasing and expanding upon Gaṅgādharabhaṭṭa's earlier commentary. Here are the options that Mathurānāth Śāstrī presents (he first focuses on the phrase *hariāla-maṇḍaia-muhī*, "face adorned with yellow paint"):

> (1) The mouth of the hemp field's entrance path is adorned with a group of yellow monkeys, and because there are no people around, it is indicated as a meeting place. (2) A girlfriend suggests to the heroine with the phrase "face which is adorned . . . " that, "just as the hemp field has a decorated face, so should you . . . adorn yourself and perform an erotic dance." (3) The act of lifting up the face is indicated by the phrase "head bent down," that is, "having bent down your face, why do you stand here? Look at my gestures." (4) Since the ripened rice field can still be a meeting place (that is, the rice has not yet been harvested), some woman whose meeting place is this rice field is mocked for her crying by some other woman whose habits are derisive.

The above passage indicates that, unlike the "fixed" interpretive modes of reading propounded for Sanskrit and Tamil poetry, *dhvani* theory allows room for readerly invention and even readerly "chaos." *Dhvani* appears to undermine the notion of convention, as well as the very idea of literary competence. The commentaries on the *Gāthāsaptaśatī* represent a "demand for sense"[34] but also seem to underscore the idea that language and meaning are things that will always outrun the grasp of the reader.[35] *Dhvani* desystematizes the more regular and classically accepted modes of reading Sanskrit and especially Prākrit poetry, explaining the variance in interpretation that extends far beyond mere double entendre. Perhaps *dhvani* most accurately describes the act of reading. It certainly accounts for the shadings of words and the different quavers of resonance for each poetic context.

Jonathan Culler has written that it is "difficult to secure agreement about what should count as a "proper understanding" of a text. . . . A work which is read differently in two periods will furnish the most decisive evidence about a system of operative conventions. . . . A comparison of old and new readings will shed light on changes in the institution of literature."[36] In the following three chapters, I will consider each "institution" separately, providing comparisons of *śāstraic* ("old") and commentatorial (relatively "new") readings for poems in Old Tamil, Sanskrit, and Māhārāṣṭrī Prākrit, in that order.

3

Reading Tamil *Cañkam* Poetry

In this chapter and in the two that follow, I have constructed brief histories of reading and interpreting love poems selected from the anthologies discussed in my introduction for each language, incorporating material from rhetorical texts and commentaries written as early as the second century B.C.E. and as recently as 1957, when Nārāyaṇacāmi Aiyar's extensive commentary on *Naṟṟiṇai* was first published. Defined in semiotic terms, the shifting, changing "signifieds" are the focus of these histories, not the more static, fixed "signifiers."

The construction of such a history for the Tamil poems presents a unique and rather difficult but interesting problem. Compared to commentarial literature attached to the Sanskrit and Prākrit anthologies, there is a stunning dearth of this material for Tamil. The page is all but blank until the modern period, save for a surviving commentary on *Aiñkuṟunūṟu,* which is repeatedly described by historians of Tamil literature as "old" and "anonymous." There is also an "old anonymous" commentary available on *Akanāṉūṟu* for the first ninety verses, though "commentary" is hardly the word to use in this case, since the materials that have survived are basically marginalia, or *kuṟippurai* ("annotations").[1] The commentary on *Aiñkuṟunūṟu* is lacking in any real detail—it provides a basic gloss—and is heavily supplemented by U. Vē. Cāminātaiyar's commentary, which was first published in Madras in 1902.[2] There is only one good modern commentary on *Naṟṟiṇai.* Tradition holds that Pērāciriyar (ca. thirteenth century C.E.) composed a commentary for all but twenty of the poems in *Kuṟuntokai* and that Nacciṉārkkiṉiyar took care of those remaining twenty maybe a hundred years later. However, these particular commentaries by these two thoroughgoing and sensitive critics have been lost, to our great misfortune.[3] For *Kuṟuntokai,* we can only rely on the two modern commentaries by Cāminātaiyar (first published in 1937) and Po. Vē. Cōmacuntaraṉār (first published in 1955). In light of this, I will discuss the ways in which the author(s) of the *Tolkāppiyam* have described the norms that inform *cañkam* poetry both within the broad categories of *akam* and *puṟam* and within the more finely honed articulations of the *akam* contexts, or *tiṇais.* I will then very briefly explain what I think are the reasons for the lack of post–*cañkam* period commentaries.

Akam and *Puṟam*

The *Poruḷatikāram* of the *Tolkāppiyam* categorizes all love poetry under a heading called *akam.*[4] *Akam* is half of the most basic genre division of *cañkam* poetry. The other half is *puṟam,* and it comes as no surprise that these two words are antonyms. At their most basic levels of meaning, *akam* means "inner" and *puṟam* means "outer." By extension, *akam* comes to refer to a person's "inner life." More specifically, *akam* means "love" in all its textures and hues. *Puṟam* is all that is outside *akam.* In poetics, it refers to a person's "outer life" or "public life" in the intersecting realms of politics and warfare. It must be kept in mind, however, that *akam* poems often refer to *puṟam* themes, and the *cañkam* poets, who often composed verse in both genres, drew the techniques they applied to both from the same pool of poetic convention. In fact, to use the word "genre" at all is a bit misleading. I prefer to visualize *akam* and *puṟam* as two parallel systems with components that often intersect. These intersections blur, and at times poets appear to erase any lines between them. Let us consider the following poem from *Kuṟuntokai:*

What her friend said:

You long only for his chest.
May you live long, Friend.

Don't be brokenhearted:

Like the ancient Kōcar warriors
who took an oath,
cut down King Naṉṉaṉ's[5]
fragrant mango tree,
and overran his land,

all we need now
is a little hard-hearted scheming.[6]

(*Kuṟuntokai* 73)

The above verse is spoken by the heroine's female friend. The heroine has already met with the man in secret, has engaged in intercourse with him, and is longing for another meeting and/or marriage.[7] The friend is telling the heroine to take heart and, by referring to an act of warfare (an event that would normally be described in a *puṟam* poem), suggests to the heroine that the man can be won over with a bit of bold, military-style strategy. According to N. Subrahmanian, the Kōcars were Tulu warriors famous for their bravery, for their truthfulness, and for keeping to their sworn word.[8] U. Vē. Cāminātaiyar's commentary on this poem states that chieftains of ancient Tamilnadu had *kāvaṉmarams,* "protected trees," and that the rash act of cutting down such a tree was considered tantamount to a declaration of war. So, through these indices, which are clearly *puṟam,* the lovesick heroine and her friend are going to make a pact and, as it were, "declare war" on the hero by metaphorically "cutting down *his* mango tree."

Likewise, *puṟam* poems are often overflowing with themes that would normally be found in *akam* poetry or are spoken from within the frame of an *akam* context, as in the following elegy from the *Puṟanāṉūṟu* ("Four Hundred [Poems] on *Puṟam* [Themes]"):

To Pāri's Hill

The mead jars were opened.
Rams and bulls were slaughtered; cooked.
There were renderings, flesh, and rice
in endless supply
and multiplying your wealth
which you gave out as we wanted it,
you befriended us then.

Now, since Pāri has died,
we've sunk into a mire of sorrow.
We've worshiped you and praised you,
our eyes brimming with tears.

We'll go, famed Paṟampu Hill,[9]
and seek out men
who have rights to the scented black hair
of Pāri's daughters,
their wrists stacked with engraved bangles.

(*Puṟanāṉūṟu* 113)

Here, the poet Kapilar, whose job it was to praise the chieftain Pāri, his patron, now can only praise what is left of Pāri—his hill and the memory of his generosity to the bards. At the end of the poem, Kapilar shifts his concern from elegy and praise, largely the business of *puṟam* poetry, to responsibilities that might seem more likely in an *akam* poetic context: he must now see to it that Pāri's orphaned girls[10] are suitably married.

There are definite structural parallels in the *Tolkāppiyam* itself that suggest that the relationship between *akam* and *puṟam* is to be thought of as dialogic and complementary rather than as oppositional. There are seven *puṟattiṇais* to match the seven *tiṇais* of *akam* poetry. They often share the "primary elements" (the *mutaṟporuḷs*) of time and place, and also of "mood" (the *uripporuḷs*). For example, *veṭci,* the *puṟam* context of the cattle raid, is situated as parallel to *kuṟiñci*. They share time (midnight) and place (the hill regions). They also share a mood that is clandestine. The stolen cows of *veṭci* are like the covert caresses of *kuṟiñci,* taken in secret under the covers of brush and darkness. Just as a cattle raid is a prelude to war, so *kuṟiñci* encounters are preludes to marriage.

Therefore, it would naturally follow that intertextual relationships between *akam* and *puṟam* poems are present. They seem to be especially present in *akam* poems composed on themes that have to do with absent or misbehaving lovers, and in *puṟam* poems of elegy and lament composed by bards whose patrons have either died or are no longer treating them well. The following two poems share the line *ācāku entai yāṇṭuḷaṉ kollō,* "our master who supports us—where is he now, I wonder?":

What she said:

When he said,
"I'll go, I'll go,"
I mistook it
for all his former mock departures
and I said, "Fine,
leave my side
and go away forever."

O Mother,
our master who supports us—
where is he now,
I wonder?

The place between my breasts
has filled up with tears,
has become a deep pond
where a black-legged
white heron feeds.[11]

(*Kuṟuntokai* 325)

Elegy for Atiyamāṉ Neṭumāṉ Añci[12]

If he had a little toddy, he gave it to us.
  All gone.
If he had a lot of toddy,
we sang while he drank happily.
  All gone.
If he had a little rice,
he portioned it out in many plates.
  All gone.
If he had a lot of rice,
he portioned it out in many plates.
  All gone.
He gave us all the meat along with bones.
  All gone.
Wherever spears and arrows entered, he stood firm.
  All gone.
He caressed my head which smelled of meat
with his hand which smelled of bitter orange.
  All gone.

The spear which pierced his precious chest
pierced the tongues of poets
in their subtle search for pretty words,
dimmed the poor eyes of his suppliants,
ran through the palms of beggars;
bored holes in the wide alms bowls
of minstrels both famous and great.
Our master who supports us—
where is he now, I wonder?
Now, there isn't a single bard
or a single soul to give to them.
Like a big jalap blossom full of honey
that flowers in a cool shoal
and stays there without being worn,
there are a great many who die
without giving one thing to others.[13]

(*Puṟanāṉūṟu* 235)

In spite of the obvious references to warfare and the patron–poet relationship described in this beautiful verse, we cannot help but note the veiled eroticism in the two lines *naranta nāṟun taṉ-kaiyāl / pulavu nāṟum eṉ-ṟalai taivarum* (literally, "With his hand which smelled of bitter orange/he caressed my head which smelled of meat"). This allusion is unclear, but it may point to certain class markers that Añci is transgressing by stroking her meat-scented head with a hand that smells of more delicate things.

We cannot, therefore, treat these two systems as exclusive divisions; they are as matrices in constant poetic dialogue. Each poem has shades of the other embedded in it; not only in the shared verbatim line but in the complex emotional structures present in the mode of lamentation. There is little difference in the qualities of feeling in the act of mourning an absent lover or a dead king: each offers protection and support. Instead of being mutually exclusive, *akam* and *puṟam* are mutually defining and interlocked; they exist in a seamless continuum. According to Nacciṉārkkiṉiyar's fourteenth-century commentary on the *Tolkāppiyam*, "*akam* and *puṟam* are like the inner palm of the hand and its back."[14]

Tiṇai and the Psychology of Place

In terms of the "symbology" of Tamil poetics, it is useful to think of the Tamil poem as hovering somewhere between memory and dream. In terms of memory, the poem is a structured reexperiencing of a past event in terms of present environments; as a dream, it is reality reworked and revised. The Tamil poets seem to have processed and revised their environments in much the same way that one recounts a dream, only with a more logical narrative structure and a fixed, encoded symbology. Generally speaking, psychoanalysis accepts that plans, maps, and the like are actually representations of the human body, the genitals, and so on. At times, the *cañkam* poems can make us wonder if the whole system of *tiṇai* might somehow represent feminine and masculine forms, especially when considering the forested mountains of the *kuṟiñci* context. The *kuṟiñci* flower itself blooms for the first time in its twelfth year, and it is difficult not to equate this with the onset of puberty and the beginnings of sexual desire. However, this equation is simplistic in view of the overall scheme of the Tamil *tiṇais.*

It is more useful to think of a *tiṇai* as a "symptomatic place," as in a "dream-text,"[15] and to think of the "germinal elements" (the *karu-p-poruḷs* on which the Tamil metaphoric/allegorical system is built) as the "day residues" that act as stimulants for mood, as well as for the entire poetic system. For the most part, a Tamil poem cannot really be thought of in terms of the Freudian rebus. There usually is no puzzle. In psychoanalytic terms, the actual geographical landscapes do not undergo a process of condensation per se, nor do they undergo any real process of "rethinking" or "recombination." Rather, the "recombinant" aspect of Tamil poetry has to do with the reshaping of *the human body* and its impulses, feelings, thoughts, and desires. All of this is accomplished in terms of what is outside the body. The poem is the place in which environment and body meet and can therefore be thought of not as the rebus but as a Lacanian mirror: the "outside"—the *tiṇai*—is the picture of the "self," and the poem represents the play between a poet's "feelings and the world's responding reflection of them."[16] Further, the Tamil poem is an expression of the poet's recognition of the human body's discontinuity with its environment, and perhaps it is also an expression of desire for continuity with it. What makes the *tiṇai* system a "poetics" is, in fact, a sort of "overdetermination." The composers of these poems foisted this desire outward upon environmental elements and incorporated those elements into a multilayered semiotics. In the poems, *tiṇai* becomes more than a "landscape" or poetic "gesture." It becomes an actual language—the constant repetition of *tiṇai* symbology gives it a "congruity," locking it into articulations of convention that are requisite for a full-blown rhetoric.

In many of the *cañkam* poems, there is a successful unification of imagery with the speaker's (the hero's or heroine's) body, upon which there are overlappings, overlayings, and splicings of *tiṇai* elements. Let us return to the last stanza of *Kuṟuntokai* 325, which I have translated in full above:

> The place between my breasts
> has filled up with tears,
> has become a deep pond
> where a black-legged
> white heron feeds.

The heroine of the poem describes her own tears by using two elements of the *neytal tiṇai,* that of the seashore, the "deep pond," and the "black-legged white heron." The poet, Naṉṉākaiyār, grafts these elements onto his heroine's chest, literally marking her body with two of the landscape features of the *neytal* context. The ponds of *neytal* are often salty, brackish places; the salt of the heroine's tears is in synecdochic correspondence with the salt of the seaside pond. The heron stands for the woman's lover; the fish upon which the heron is feeding represent her and also other women, a common convention in this context. In *Kuṟuntokai* 334, cited in the preceding section, the poet Iḷampūtaṉār uses an extended *uḷḷuṟai-y-uvamam* in the indented stanza to evoke the heroine's physical discomfort. But perhaps the most striking example of the relationship between body and environment is *Kuṟuntokai* 290, composed by Kalporu Ciṟunuraiyār, who took his name from the image in the stunning simile around which he constructed this poem ("he who sang of a streak of foam dashing against stones"):

What she said:

Those who tell me
to bear my love:

Don't they know about love,
or are they that strong?

Since I can't see my lover,
my heart swells
with hidden sorrow
and like a flood in spate
turning to a streak of foam
as it dashes against stones,

slowly,
slowly, I turn to nothing.

(*Kuṟuntokai* 290)

Here, the heroine complains to her friend about people who tell her to bear her love—according to Cāminātaiyar's commentary, these people include anyone who "cannot understand the nature of desire,"[17] probably townsfolk and her own family members. Her lover is absent for some reason. The heroine is anxious for his return and is probably exhibiting the physical signs of separation: it is likely that she has turned pale and appears disheveled and emaciated. Her people are worried and tell her to just be strong and endure the unendurable. The heroine speaks of the grief that surges thick in her heart, comparing herself to a swell of water that diminishes as it crashes against rocks. She is so overwhelmed by her longing that she fears that it will consume her; that she will simply stop being. The last line of the poem, *mella mella-v-illākutumē* ("slowly, slowly, I turn to nothing") reflects the repetitive motion of *neytal* waves. The word *illākutum* is a fascinating juncture of two verbs that mean "not to be" (verbal root *il*) and "to be" or "to become" (verbal root *āku*). The elements of the *neytal* context figuratively swell up, consume, and nearly destroy the heroine as she grieves in her lover's absence.

It seems that some of the *caṅkam* poets have preferred to manipulate *tiṇai* imagery in a more indexical sort of way. Many of the longer, more "narrative" *Naṟṟiṇai* poems have a somewhat less sophisticated, more mise-en-scène feel to them. In many of these poems, it is clear that the characters are speaking as exemplars of an occupation and are a part of the actual world of the poetic *tiṇai* that frames their words. For instance, the anonymous poet of the following poem has literally imbued his two female characters with *neytal*-ness: they work on the docks as fishmongers, and their very bodies reek of fish. This poem also presents a bit of an interpretive problem. Although the elements are clearly *neytal,* and A. Nārāyaṇacāmi Aiyar classifies this poem as such in his 1957 commentary, I suspect that this is actually a *kuṟiñci* verse in which the poet has used *neytal* imagery to evoke the difficulties of the situation. In this very unusual poem, the speaker, the female friend of the heroine, reproaches the hero for his interest. But the poem could also be interpreted as a "strategy" to make the man jealous, forcing him to prize the heroine more highly and to act more quickly to marry her:

What her friend said (to discourage him):

This girl
  lives in a small
  pleasant village
  near the shore,
  a daughter of fishermen
  who pierce and stir up the waters
  of the big blue sea
  as they kill fish.

And you?
  You're from that old market town
  where long banners shiver
  in the breeze,
  a beloved son
  of a rich man
  with fast chariots.

What is your beauty to us,
  who want the dried meat
  we slice from fat sharks
  as we sit and scare off
  flocks of birds?

We reek of fish,
so get ready to leave.

The good little lives
that we make for ourselves
from the fruits of the sea
are not like yours,
and among us, too,
there are fine men to be had.

(*Naṟṟiṇai* 45)

At the beginning of the poem, the female friend directly addresses the love-struck hero, clearly pointing out to him the class differences between his family and the heroine's family. The third stanza is the one in which *uḷḷuṟai-y-uvamam* is employed. The heroine's girlfriend assumes that the hero is a predator, another marauding bird to be scared off from a tender scrap of *neytal* fish (i.e., the heroine herself).

There are also explicit relationships between the physical surroundings of *tiṇai* and the emotional and personal traits of the characters. Each *tiṇai* has its own "psychology," as it were, defined by the *uripporuḷs* that I discussed above. To continue with *neytal* imagery, the overriding *uripporuḷ* of this *tiṇai* is *irañkal*, "lamenting the lover's absence." There is usually some sort of separation involved, joined with an overlay of impatience, restlessness, and suspicion. The "primary elements" (the *mutaṟporuḷs*) are the seacoast (for place) and the sunrise (for time): for season, the *Tolkāppiyam* tells us that this can happen at any time of year. So, lamentation is seasonless. It is very interesting that sunrise is prescribed for the time of day—the poems often depict a woman waking in the morning and finding that her lover had not returned the previous night. The "germinal elements" (the *karupporuḷs*) are mostly things that shake and rustle—the branches of *neytal* trees are often described as "swaying" or "shaking." The lands are watery, salty marshes, and the animals that populate this *tiṇai* are mostly dangerous and predatory: herons, sharks, and crocodiles dominate the scene. Therefore, the general evocation of this context is one of unease. Nothing seems to be on solid ground, and everything is threatening, brackish, and uncomfortable. The following poem, composed by Veṇpūti, demonstrates one way in which a heroine has to bury her chastity and sorrow, depositing them together in a *neytal* marsh:

> *What she said (her lover not having returned for many days):*
>
> As for me,
> I am here.
>
> My virtue lies
> with boundless grief
> in a salt marsh.
>
> He is in his town,
>
> and our secret
> has become gossip
> in common places.
>
> (*Kuṟuntokai* 97)

The above poem serves as an excellent example of the ways in which a character can splice or graft his or her emotions onto the actual landscape. The heroine's grief in separation and her *nalaṉ* (her Goodness with a capital "G": her virginity) are left to rot secretly in a fetid marsh while her lover stays comfortably at home. She is bereft of him as well as her own chastity; she can grieve for neither publicly and resigns her feelings to the land, while the secret of their love becomes grist for the local gossip mill.

Another poem, this one by Perumpākkaṉ, serves to illustrate the ways in which the *neytal* elements are used in the technique of *uḷḷuṟai-y-uvamam* to evoke disturbing feelings of unsteadiness, suspicion, and predation:

> *What her friend said to him, quoting the heroine:*
>
> Listen, Friend,
> and live long.
>
> > Because a fine-winged heron
> > balanced on a swaying mastwood branch
> > spurns the tiny fish

in the wide salt marsh
and craves the blue lilies
fragrant with nectar
in the fields with its spears of rice,

when you see that cool and handsome man,
don't chide him.
Don't dare to ask him
if it's right for him
to leave that girl with the bangles
when she's in a state like this.

(*Kuṟuntokai* 296)

The *uḷḷuṟai-y-uvamam* is all in the indented second stanza. The heron represents the hero, and his infidelity is indicated through the "swaying mastwood branch" upon which the heron is standing. The "tiny fish" is the heroine, and she again alludes to her lover's fickleness by saying that what he craves are other, inappropriate women, who are the "blue lilies fragrant with nectar in the fields with its spears of rice." Herons are fish eating, and for them to crave lilies is unnatural. The heron has also left its usual habitat for a rice field. The *neytal* flower itself, the blue lily, the emblem of this particular *tiṇai,* is used to represent the other women.

U. Vē. Cāminātaiyar and the Birth of the Modern Tamil Commentary

In the above paragraphs, I have described some of the basic elements of *cañkam* poetry by drawing on the prescriptions of the *Tolkāppiyam,* by relying on several modern commentaries to unravel some of the poetic correspondences in the poems, and by turning to modern psychoanalytic theory as a plausible method for interpretation. Sadly missing from this picture are any medieval commentaries on the Tamil anthologies, probably because in South India, commentarial effort was largely a sectarian enterprise. Why should theologians waste their breath on secular literature that lacks in any perceivable devotional or didactic value? *Cañkam* imagery was appropriated by poets working in later devotional genres, to be sure, but the only real attempt that we know of in which *cañkam* poems have been interpreted and commented on in a significant way is in Nakkīraṉār's lengthy, dense, and highly idiosyncratic commentary on an eighth-century reworking of Tamil literary convention, *Iṟaiyaṉār Aka-p-poruḷ*.[18] Nakkīraṉār's attempt to demonstrate the religious value in *cañkam* erotic relationships is superficial, at best. He makes a rather vain attempt, in my estimation, to rethink secular *cañkam* poetry within a Śaiva devotional framework. Aside from this, this particular page in the history of *cañkam* literature is all but blank until the late nineteenth century with U. Vē. Cāminātaiyar's "rediscovery" of the *cañkam* anthologies in the corner of a South Indian monastery.

U. Vē. Cāminātaiyar (1855–1942), already a prodigious scholar at the age of twenty-five and a known expert in medieval Tamil texts, was teaching in a college at Kumbakonam and was sent by his *maṭam* (the Śaiva religious institution to which he was affiliated) to meet the new Munsiff, Irāmacuvāmi Mutaliyār. Mutaliyār came from an old zamindari family and was a bit of a renaissance man, knowing Tamil, Sanskrit, and music. He began to question Cāminātaiyar about the texts he knew and remained unimpressed after listening to Cāminātaiyar's lengthy bibliography of *antātis, purāṇas, piḷḷai-t-tamiḻs,*[19] and the *Kamparāmāyāṇa*. Cāminātaiyar recounts this interview with Mutaliyār in his autobiography, *Eṉ Carittiram:*

> Irāmacuvāmi Mutaliyār said, "Fine," but then asked me, "Is that all?" That made me very unhappy. He seemed to have contempt even for the *Kamparāmāyaṇa*. What arrogance! That is how I had reasoned it out. What was there to say after that? But he wasn't going to let me off the hook. He then asked me, "It is a fine thing that you've studied all these old books, but have you read any of the *ancient texts?*"[20]

Cāminātaiyar had no inkling of what Mutaliyār was referring to. Mutaliyār then asked Cāminātaiyar if he had studied *Cīvaka Cināmaṇi,*[21] *Maṇimēkalai,* or *Cilappatikāram*. Cāminātaiyar had to admit that not only had he not studied them, he had not even *heard* of them! Mutaliyār then gave Cāminātaiyar a copy of *Cīvaka Cintāmaṇi*, which marked Cāminātaiyar's entry into the study of Jaina literature. More importantly, Cāminātaiyar began to wonder about other ancient works that might have escaped his notice. He returned to the manuscript library at his *maṭam* at Tiruvāvaṭuturai. He writes:

> I duly began to rummage through bundles of old palm leaves. All of the leaves were badly decayed and stuck together. Someone had attached a slip to one of the bundles which read, "A collection of palm leaves *(ēṭṭu-t-tokai)*. These look like *cankam* texts." I examined this bundle and found it to contain manuscripts of *Naṟṟiṇai* and other *cankam* texts.[22]

The bundle, in fact, contained six of the eight *cankam* anthologies, of which Cāminātaiyar knew from a passing reference in an old verse. Cāminātaiyar explains that there had been a spelling error on that identifying slip of paper. It should have read *eṭṭu-t-tokai* ("eight anthologies") instead of *ēṭṭu-t-tokai*, which could refer to any collection of *ēṭus*, or palm leaves.[23]

Cāminātaiyar went on to edit and publish five of the eight *cankam* anthologies, writing lucid commentaries on each. He drew his inspiration for the structure of these commentaries from a number of sources, some truly remarkable. When Cāminātaiyar began to edit the *Puṟanāṉūṟu*, he had the good fortune of finding a manuscript with an old commentary for the first 260 verses. The commentary was patchy but identified the *tiṇai* and *tuṟai* for most of the poems. While visiting in the home of a friend, Cāminātaiyar noticed that he was holding a particularly large English book in his hand. He writes in his autobiography:

> "What book is that?" I asked. "It's the *Bible*," he replied. I said, "But the *Bible* is a small book, isn't it? This one is very big." "This is a special edition of it in which all events and principal words are systematically arranged . . . with cross-references. It's called a 'concordance' in English," he said, showing me some selections. There, I saw various types of numbers, as well as pictures of the compiler and his assistant. I asked, "What's the use of this?"[24]

The friend went on to explain to Cāminātaiyar that this helped in determining the correct forms of words and in keeping the text relatively error-free. At the end of their meeting, Cāminātaiyar, who was unable to read a word of English, had decided that "here was a new way to conduct my work on the *Puṟanāṉūṟu*."[25] Hence, the birth of the Tamil "critical edition," which occurred at the intersection of many avenues of tradition—Jaina texts, Śaiva scholarship, and an imprint left by the shape of a Christian English-language biblical concordance.

When Cāminātaiyar published his edition of *Cīvaka Cintāmaṇi* in 1888, he was harshly criticized for it. Letters and pamphlets were circulated that condemned Cāminātaiyar, "a person who owed everything to a Śaiva *maṭam*,"[26] for associating himself with the publication of a Jaina text. So, once again, sectarian prejudices were getting in the way and, by 1905, so were the Madras police. Jay Singh, a police official who happened to be Cāminātaiyar's neighbor in Madras, was "outraged by the romantic [*sic*][27] descriptions of women"[28] in certain passages of Tamil poetry, and wanted to burn the entire lot. It is reported that Cāminātaiyar convinced him that it was wrong to do so by telling him that if he did this to *cañkam* literature, "we would have to dump the whole of Tamil and Sanskrit literature into the sea and smash all temple statues and idols."[29]

The above paragraphs have made it fairly clear that there was a sort of "textual hierarchy" established by Vaiṣṇava and Śaiva scholars, and, in a sense, it seems that *cañkam* poetry was assigned the lowest possible value. Not only was it considered "pornographic," but it was also "bad" because it was deemed somehow "secular" and therefore undeserving as an object of scholarly discourse. Colonial period archival records bear this out. In records held by the Tamilnadu state archives in Madras, it is apparent that the British colonial administration at Fort Saint George, the Department of Public Education in particular, supported the ranking of texts that had been made by Hindu scholars. The Christian "ethic" of studying texts that had requisite amounts of "moral value" agreed very neatly with the decisions made by local Tamil *paṇḍits* on what sorts of texts were acceptable for study in the local schools, as well as what was deemed fit for translation into English.[30] Indeed, save for Cāminātaiyar's pre-Independence commentaries on the *cañkam* and epic texts, no other commentaries were written until after Independence, and then only after the Tamil nationalist movement was in full swing. It was this very nationalist movement that dampened religious conflict in Tamilnadu. Suddenly, it was much more important to be a "Tamil" than a Śaiva Hindu or a Jain. North Indian customs and languages (Sanskrit and Hindi, in particular) became the common "enemy." These phenomena were all a result of the so-called Tamil renaissance, which U. Vē. Cāminātaiyar had practically created all on his own.

4

Reading the Sanskrit *Amaruśataka*

When foregrounded against the diverse categories of Sanskrit literary genres, it becomes apparent that the *Amaruśataka* represents a part of a distinct movement away from the traditional mythic materials and categories that earlier Sanskrit poets and dramatists, such as Kālidāsa, drew upon. As V. Raghavan, Siegfried Lienhard, and others have pointed out, the *Amaruśataka* "is really a continuation in Sanskrit of the Prākrit tradition of love poetry begun in Hāla's *Gāthāsaptaśatī;* with the exception of a few interpolated poems by other authors, it is the first anthology of short erotic poems in Sanskrit."[1]

It is my primary strategy here to discuss semiotic and psychological aspects of certain individual poems in the *Amaruśataka,* and also to apply my own readerly responses and reflexes to the interpretations of a number of Sanskrit critics. I will primarily be relying on the following works: (1) the writings of Ānandavardhana in his late ninth-century[2] text, the *Dhvanyāloka,* coupled with Abhinavagupta's *Locana* commentary composed a century later, (2) Dhanika's *Avaloka* commentary, probably composed in the late tenth century[3] to accompany Dhanañjaya's *Daśarūpa,* a text on dramaturgy from the same period, and (3) Mammaṭa's *Kāvyaprakāśa,* a comprehensive work on rhetoric from approximately the late eleventh century.[4] I will also discuss the interpretations of the text by its two major commentators, namely, Arjunavarmadeva (ca. 1200 C.E.)[5] and Vemabhūpāla (ca. 1400 C.E.).[6] It is often instructive to read Vemabhūpāla after having read Arjunavarmadeva—it is apparent that Vemabhūpāla had composed his commentary to serve as a "corrective" to Arjunavarmadeva's work.

The authors of the first three works seem to have greatly admired the verses from the *Amaruśataka*. Dhanika employs by far the greatest number of Amaru citations, quoting verses from the anthology in twenty-four separate instances. The citations are limited to the second and fourth sections of the work, and they are primarily used to illustrate the different types of Sanskrit *nāyikās* or heroines (section 2) and *vyabhicāribhāvas* or transitory feelings (section 4). However, the citations themselves are given in a very cursory way, with little or no introduction or explanation as to how the verses illustrate a particular behavior or feeling. After all, the *Daśarūpa* and Dhanika's commentary are not concerned with poetics in the same sense in which Ānandavardhana and Mammaṭa clearly were. Instead, their concern was with dramatic representation. Dhanañjaya's focus was on the exposition of dramatic categories, and his text is a deliberate simplification, written in a very efficient "shorthand," of some of the major principles espoused in Bharata's *Nāṭyaśāstra*. Although it is clear that Dhanika was aware of the work of Ānandavardhana, he did nothing with it other than cite five of Ānandavardhana's stanzas.[7] Though Dhanika's lack of analysis is disappointing, it underscores the fact that many Sanskrit poets composed their works, no matter of what length, with an eye toward dramatic portrayal. The Amaru poems in particular rely heavily on descriptions of costume and gesture to convey specific sentiments; hence, the appeal to critics such as Dhanika. For instance, Dhanika appends *Amaruśataka* 31 to *Daśarūpa* 2.27 as an example of an *abhisārikā*, a *nāyikā* who, by Dhanañjaya's definition, is "lovesick and goes after her lover, or makes him come after her." This definition is immediately followed by nothing more than a simple *yathā-amaruśatake* ("as in the *Amaruśataka*") and the poem:

> You've strung your breasts
> with a rattling rope of pearls,
> tied a jangling belt
> around those deadly hips
> and clinking jeweled anklets
> on both your feet.

So, stupid,
  if you run off to your lover like this,
banging all these drums,
  then why
do you shudder with all this fear
  and look up, down,
in every direction?

Ānandavardhana, Abhinavagupta, and Mammaṭa cite *Amaruśataka* verses with far less frequency, but, by and large, they have far more intriguing things to say about the poems in the course of their literary expositions. Ānandavardhana's primary focus is not on dramatic representation, but on the sheer aesthetic value of language and the conveyance of meaning; in other words, with the signifying and aesthetic capacities of language in general. By Ānandavardhana's time, it was generally accepted that a word possessed two levels of meaning:[8] *abhidhā* ("designation," the literal sense of a word) and *lakṣaṇā* ("indication," the indirect or figurative sense of a word). Daniel Ingalls further explains:

> In addition to these two powers, the school of ritualists founded by Kumārila held that there existed a third power which furnished a "final meaning" to the sentence as a whole. They called this the *tātparyaśakti,* and defended its reality against their opponents, the Prābhākara ritualists, who claimed that the denotative force in each word kept on operating until at the conclusion of the sentence it worked automatically in harmony with the other words.[9]

But none of these seemed to satisfy or encompass Ānandavardhana's notion that a word's *vyañjakatva,* its "suggestive-ness," was, of all of a word's semantic powers, "the most valuable for poetic expression."[10] He termed this power *dhvani,* "overtone," "echo," "resonance." Ānandavardhana thereby brought to literary criticism in Sanskrit a new, original, and critically generative focus without summarily rejecting the writings of his predecessors, since the "building blocks" of the *Dhvanyāloka* include *rasa* theory and the ideas of earlier critics and linguistic theorists.

Unlike Dhanika, Ānandavardhana (and Abhinavagupta, the main commentator on the *Dhvanyāloka)* addressed critical questions about poetry and poetics head-on, recognizing that there was much more to Sanskrit and Prākrit poetry than its dramatic elements and representational potential. Ānandavardhana and Abhinavagupta asked and answered the basic critical questions of *why* and *how* a poem is good or bad. What resulted was sophisticated analysis, as well as works that set the standard for much of the later critical and commentarial writing, as well as later poetic production.

The verses of the *Amaruśataka* are cited in six different instances in the *Dhvanyāloka* and the accompanying *Locana* commentary to illustrate a variety of critical ideas and categories. For example, in his commentary following *Dhvanyāloka* 1.4, Abhinavagupta quotes *Amaruśataka* 23 in the middle of a long exposition on *rasa, bhāva,* and the *ābhāsa* (the "semblance" or "improper variety") of both, as an illustration of *bhāva-praśama,* or the "quelling of emotion," writing that "the very breaking of one's train of thought" is something that "especially refreshes the heart":

> Lying on the same bed,
> backs to each other,
> without any answers,
> holding their breath,
>
> even though making up
> with each other
> was in their heart,
> both guarded their pride,
>
> but slowly,
> each looked sideways,
> glances mingled
> and the quarrel
> exploded in laughter,
> in enfolding embraces.

Abhinavagupta adds, "This [verse] is an illustration of the breaking of pride characterized by jealous anger," meaning that the delight of the poem resides in the sudden and surprising erasure of anger by the laughter and intimacy at the end of the verse.

There is another, more interesting quotation in Ānandavardhana's second chapter. At *Dhvanyāloka* 2.14, Ānandavardhana makes a case against the employment of sequential alliteration *(anuprāsa)* in *śṛṅgāra* poetry because it renders a poem "labored" and not a "discloser" *(prakāśakaḥ)* of *śṛṅgāra-rasa.* He makes an identical case against the use of paranomastic alliteration *(yamaka)* at 2.15. He writes: "When desire characterizes a suggestive poem, the employment of *yamaka,* etc., is a mistake even though the poet is skilled, in the case of *vipralambha* poems especially." What Ānandavardhana is doing, in essence, is slowly building a "less-is-more," uncluttered aesthetic for *śṛṅgāra* poetry in general by advising against the overuse of *alaṃkāras* ("ornaments," "rhetorical figures") of any kind. At *Dhvanyāloka* 2.16, he qualifies this prescription even further, writing: "A rhetorical figure which might be composed while focussed on *rasa* and not brought about by means of a separate effort is allowable in *dhvani* poetry," meaning that if a poet's mind is fixed on the production of *rasa,* a rhetorical figure that might ensue while the poet is properly focussed will not detract from the poem's beauty. Ānandavardhana expands this notion a bit more, writing that even if the figure is "extraordinary in its execution" *(niṣpattau āścarya-bhūtaḥ),* it still may be used in the type of poem in which the movement from the literal to the suggested meaning goes unnoticed. The figure must always remain in a position that is subordinate to the *rasa.* Here, Ānandavardhana quotes *Amaruśataka* 81:

> You've erased the tracery
> on your cheek
> by covering it with your palm.
>
> Your sighs have kissed away
> the juice of your lower lip,
> tasty as nectar
>
> and at every instant,
> the tear that's stuck in your throat
> is making your sloping breasts tremble.
>
> Unkind girl,
> anger has become your lover,
> not I.

Ānandavardhana has ostensibly cited this verse here to demonstrate that, although a verse might contain an elaborate figure, it can serve *rasa* rather than overwhelm it. The verse above does not contain *anuprāsa* or *yamaka,* but the poet *has* employed a type of metaphor, or *rūpaka,* that the commentator Arjunavarmadeva identifies as *apahnuti,* "a figure in which the subject of comparison (here, the girl's anger) is portrayed as possessing a quality which in nature belongs to the object of comparison (the lover)."[11] As commentator Vemabhūpāla points out, the *nāyikā*'s anger is doing all the things a lover would usually do.[12] In his essay which follows this example, Ānandavardhana states: "Only those special utterances—that is, rhetorical figures such as *rūpakas*—can disclose [*rasa*] and are therefore not exterior to it, but *yamakas* and other such difficult figures are." Ānandavardhana then summarily dismisses the use of such figures in love poetry altogether, since they completely distract the reader from *dhvani,* and therefore, *rasa.*

At *Dhvanyāloka* 2.18–19, Ānandavardhana further qualifies the use of figures such as *rūpaka*—those figures which are acceptable as disclosers of *rasa*—by pleading a case for understatement. He writes: "[The poet] whose heart is focussed solely on the conveyance of *rasa* will not wish to carry [a figure] out to excess." He then quotes *Amaruśataka* 9:

> Angry,
> she tied him up fast
> in the snares
> of the dainty,
> trembling vines
> of her arms.
>
> At night,
> she led him to her place,
> paraded him
> before her friends,
> and stammered,
> "If you do this again . . . "
>
> She hints
> at his rotten behavior

with sweet words
and the lucky man,
bent on denial,
laughs as he's hit
by the crying girl.

Ānandavardhana then finishes his thought, writing: "Here, the *rūpaka* is hinted at but not completed, resulting in the full development of *rasa*."

In the *Locana* section that follows, Abhinavagupta demonstrates just how absurd the poem would become if the *rūpaka* were carried out to excess by demonstrating what the poet could have done but chose not to do: "If [the poet] were to carry out fully the *rūpaka* of [the *nāyikā's*] creeper-like arms as being a binding fetter, then the beloved woman would be a female hunter, the bedroom would be a jail, a cage, or the like, and thus, it would be most inappropriate."

The above examples begin to delineate for us the particular poetic preferences of Ānandavardhana and Abhinavagupta. They also begin to show us why and how the poems of the *Amaruśataka* are well crafted in matters of poetic language and in the use of figurative speech, not just as exemplars of mechanical dramatic representation. What was good to Ānandavardhana and Abhinavagupta was allusion: the thing half-done, the utterance half-said, the trope half-developed. These seem to have held much more charm for these two skillful critics than poems that displayed elaborate figurative pyrotechnics. The allusive powers of words and meanings, as captured by Ānandavardhana conceptually in *dhvani* as a critical idea, were the only means to convey *rasa,* and the examples that he and Abhinavagupta have cited from the *Amaruśataka* certainly seem to have borne this out beautifully.

Perhaps some two centuries after the composition of the *Dhvanyāloka,* Mammaṭa composed the *Kāvyaprakāśa,* a compendious text that is quite literally a summary of everything in Sanskrit that had to do with literature up to that point. Mammaṭa omitted only dramaturgical material, perhaps because Dhanañjaya had produced the *Dāśarūpa* a century earlier. By this time, the lines between what constituted "drama" on the one hand and "lyric poetry" on the other were becoming much more clearly drawn. Mammaṭa was a firm proponent of the ideas of Ānandavardhana and Abhinavagupta, and his

Kāvyaprakāśa, really a textbook rather than an original work of criticism, includes chapters on *rasa, dhvani, alaṃkāras, dōṣas* ("faults"), and *guṇas* ("qualities").

Mammaṭa cites poems from the *Amaruśataka* in fifteen different instances throughout the body of the *Kāvyaprakāśa.* Unfortunately for us, like Dhanika, he had very little to say about the poems themselves and, in most instances, has only very mechanically reproduced them as hackneyed and predictable examples of very basic ideas. For example, an Amaru poem (number 49) is cited as an illustration of a *vyabhicāribhāva* at 4.28, and at 4.29, four verses are listed—without explanation—as examples of *sambhoga-śṛṅgāra-rasa* (numbers 82 and 27) and *vipralambha-śṛṅgāra-rasa* (numbers 29 and 35). Verses 23 and 26 are listed in an identical fashion at 4.36 as illustrations of the quieting of an emotion *(bhāva)* and the onset of one. The verses, all in all, are well chosen but are employed in an encyclopedic way, which is rather disappointing.

However, Mammaṭa really begins to shine as a sensitive reader of poetry a bit later on in his fourth chapter. His citations become less mechanical and disclose an interest in poetry that seems to be more linguistically and grammatically grounded. For instance, at 4.43 he quotes *Amaruśataka* 7 as an example of how "*rasa* and things like it [are found] in parts of words, in style, and in letters, as well":

likhannāste bhūmiṃ bahiravanataḥ prāṇadayito
nirāhārāḥ sakhyaḥ satataruditocchūnanayanāḥ
parityaktaṃ sarvaṃ hasitapaṭhitaṃ pañjaraśukais
tavāvasthā ceyaṃ visṛja, kaṭhine! mānam adhunā

The love of your life
sits outside, downcast,
scratching on the ground.
Your friends won't eat—
their eyes are puffy
from all their crying.

The pet parrots have quit
all their silly recitations,
and just look at the shape you're in.

Hard-hearted Girl,
get rid of this jealousy
now.

Mammaṭa's short but perceptive explanation follows:

> In this case, [the poet has chosen to use] *likhan,* "is scratching," rather than *likhati,* "scratches;" *āste,* "sits," rather than *āsitaḥ,* "was seated"—meaning that he will sit until [the *nāyikā*] is completely appeased; and *bhūmim,* "ground" declined in the accusative rather than "ground" declined in the locative, [indicating that the *nāyaka*] is scratching something on the ground without his conscious attention.

This shows us that Mammaṭa has understood the poet's subtle manipulation of certain temporal aspects of verbs in the first two cases, and the poetic nuances of declension in the last, and how these minutiae can add to the disclosure of the *rasa* of this verse, which, according to Vemabhūpāla, is *vipralambha-śṛṅgāra* due to jealous anger.[13] The poet's use of continuative verbal forms (that is, by choosing a present participial form of *likh* and a continuative present-tense form of *ās*) helps to disclose the *rasa* by sustaining the *nāyaka's* actions throughout the verse in a temporal fashion. And, we can surmise that what Mammaṭa is suggesting is that scratching *on* the ground, rather than *in* it, portrays the *nāyaka's* distracted lack of purpose, showing how upset he is by his lover's unspoken jealous accusations.

In his seventh chapter, Mammaṭa cites *Amaruśataka* 40, which I discuss at length below, as an illustration of how the *doṣa* or "blemish" called *nyūna-pada,* "the lack of a word," can sometimes actually become a *guṇa,* or something that qualitatively "adds" to the poem. We have to assume that Mammaṭa must be referring to the direct quotation of the *nāyikā's* orgasmic cries in the first half of the third line, *mā, mā, mānada! Māti mām alam!* ("Don't, don't, thief of my pride! Don't! Too much! Enough for me!") The woman's words, broken and half-said in pleasure, are what disclose the *rasa* of this verse, *sambhoga-śṛṅgāra*. However, something as obvious as this becomes a problem when we move from the discussion of these verses in literary *śāstras*—which show *how* poems convey meaning—into a discussion of commentaries, which are more interested in *what* these poems mean.

Desire in Interpretation

When we turn to the two major commentaries on the *Amaruśataka*, we encounter in the interpretations a different and somehow more qualified reading of sensuality. I have already remarked that both of the major commentators tend to favor a *vipralambha* interpretation for the poems in this collection, however graphic or explicit a poem may be. It seems that in general, poems that are labeled in their headnotes as *kaver uktiḥ*, as spoken directly by the poet in his role as a third-person narrator of an erotic event, are the ones that are interpreted as true *sambhoga* verses. But, strangely enough, when the words of an explicit verse are placed in the mouth of a lover, both writers, Arjunavarmadeva especially, frame these poems inside a *vipralambha* context in their introductory headnotes and in their following interpretive glosses. The most extreme case of this latter brand of interpretation involves verse 40:

Her breasts
were dwarfed
in a tight embrace.
The hair of her body
bristled with desire.

That cloth
on her glorious hips
melted away
in the heat
of the moment
and with weak words
she urged me,

"Don't, don't,
thief of my pride,
don't. For me,
it's more than enough."

Then, I don't know—
was she asleep,
or dead?
Did she merge
with my heart?
Did she dissolve
into nothing?

(*Amaruśataka* 40)

Now, at least at first glance, this verse could be interpreted as nothing other than a verse evoking *sambhoga-śṛṅgāra-rasa,* and the commentator Vemabhūpāla tersely concurs. His headnote simply states *nayakoktiḥ* ("a *nāyaka's,* or male character's, address"), identifies the *rasa* as *sambhoga-śṛṅgāra,* and the *nāyikā,* or female character, as a *parakīyā kanyā,* "a young girl who belongs to another,"[14] a typical identification for the heroine in verses of this graphic a nature.

Arjunavarmadeva's headnote, on the other hand, is quite unexpected. It reads: "A man who is separated from his lover, and who is skilled in sport, with his mind fixed on her alone, contemplates all aspects of a *māninī-nāyikā,*" that is, a woman given to pride or haughtiness, or, more specifically to Sanskrit poetry, a woman who is quick to anger during a love spat and needs instant appeasement.[15]

Arjunavarmadeva's reading raises a very interesting problem in interpretation. Obviously, this is a *śṛṅgāra-rasa* verse, but of which type, *sambhoga* or *vipralambha?* What is it that determines the nuance? The verse itself or the context inside which it is understood by the reader? If the more general principles of *rasa* theory are adhered to—that is, if it is accepted that *rasa* is what is experienced by the audience or reader—then, obviously, the latter is true, and we can say that the poem is capable of conveying either *sambhoga* or *vipralambha-śṛṅgāra,* or even both at once, depending on the inclinations of its audience or reader.

It was certainly my first instinct to dismiss immediately Arjunavarmadeva's interpretation as far-fetched and evasive, and to accept Vemabhūpāla's simpler explanation. However, the more I considered this case, the more perplexed and fascinated I became with Arjunavarmadeva's interpretation. In effect, this commentator has stripped the poem of its sexuality—its "pleasure," if you will—and has turned it and the characters it portrays into objects for the sheer delectation of its consumers. If we wish to think of this poem in terms of Roland Barthes's rich dialogics of pleasure and desire,[16] the commentator has transformed the poem from a pleasure-giving object into an object that elicits desire, which is precisely what a critic of the *rasa* school would be expected to do, in order to remove the audience from the direct experience of the *bhāva* ("emotion") into the aesthetic mode of *rasa*.

Desire, characterized by a loss that is softened by the knowledge of the eventual restoration of the lost object, would have been ultimately familiar to a connoisseur of Sanskrit poetry. It is this very distinction that differentiates *vipralambha-śṛṅgāra* from *karuṇa-rasa* (the "compassionate" *rasa* that is evoked from the *bhāva* of *śoka* or "grief"). In most *sāhitya-śāstras*, we find that if the loss of a lover or loved one is permanent, the *rasa* is that of *karuṇa;* if the loss is merely temporary, it is then interpreted as *vipralambha-śṛṅgāra*.

Love poems in Sanskrit, therefore, should move from gain to loss to gain. The equation, in order to avoid *karuṇa-rasa,* must always end in gain, the ultimate goal of *śṛṅgāra*. But oddly enough, the poems are hardly ever explicitly about the goal of union or reunion. Union and reunion are nearly always implied, and rarely explicit. With the exception of verses that are directly narrated by the poet, union and reunion occur either before or after the event narrated in the poem and never during it. Union and reunion are always implied and are rarely explicit, forcing the "pleasure in the text" to a level that can only be described as supratextual.

The concept of love as *smara* or remembrance—*smara* as it encapsulates its multilayered meanings of memory and sexual love—seems to be the right word for love as it is portrayed in the *Amaruśataka*. The poems can be construed either as memories of having reached a goal or as cast in the context of loss—into a potent dialectic of having/not having. Wanting, longing, and yearning are the issues, and not the actual having. If we examine the earlier literary treatises, especially the third chapter of Ānandavardhana's *Dhvanyāloka,* we see that, even on a level as basic as that of *aucitya* ("propriety," "that which is appropriate in a poem"), *vipralambha* is preferred, and, in fact, claims a sort of preeminence over *sambhoga*.[17]

Vipralambha is a much more complicated and rich mood for portrayal than that of *sambhoga*. The varieties of *vipralambha* are incalculable, although Sanskrit poeticians have certainly attempted to quantify them. There is a beautiful tension in *vipralambha* due to its psychological dimensions. It may be the mood in the human experience that is felt with the most clarity and with the most painful sort of acuity.

What is more, if union and reunion are always present in loss, then the reverse is also true: loss is also present in union. There is always the taint of *vipralambha* in *sambhoga*, for we cannot contemplate or possess any person or object without seeing it in the light of its possible loss. There is always the recognition that the object's presence is in some way arbitrary and provisional. There is a Prākrit *gāthā*, *Gāthāsaptaśatī* 1.98, that illustrates this beautifully. A *nāyikā* says:

When he has loved me,
goes but a step away
and returns
to love me again,

for that instant,
I'm like a wife
whose husband's away,
as if he's been exiled.

As I have pointed out, Arjunavarmadeva's headnotes are often unexpected, and I have cited the most remarkable example, verse 40. Here are two more examples: the first, a couplet that comes as verse 64 in Arjunavarmadeva's recension, and the second, verse 102, with which this commentator closes the Amaru collection. Verse 64 follows below:

I don't know.

When my lover
comes to me
and says such loving things,

do all my parts
become eyes
or ears?

I must admit that I became quite frustrated when I read the headnote to this verse and the subsequent commentary. I "mistakenly" read this verse as possibly an inexperienced girl's confession to her girlfriend. But Arjunavarmadeva has stripped this verse of all of the innocence that I had perceived in it. He frames it within the context of a love quarrel with this headnote: "'In front of *us,* you talk about your anger in the extreme, but when you're in *his* presence, you become an altogether different person.' Scolded thus by her girlfriends, a certain woman defends her own faults." In other words, Arjunavarmadeva has described the girlfriends as being rather fed up with the heroine's angry plaints. They scold her for softening in her lover's presence, and the heroine then defends herself by beautifully describing the physical effect her lover has on her. By placing the verse in such a context, Arjunavarmadeva charges it with a certain tension that would not be present at all in my own reading. He also identifies the woman as a *bhāva-pragalbhā-nāyikā,* a woman who is "bold in her emotions."[18]

I would prefer to interpret this verse as the words of a young woman who is clumsy because of her inexperience and is having a difficult time maintaining her composure in front of her sweet-talking lover. She may also be puzzled by her own body's responses to the new onslaught of sexual desire she is experiencing. As I mentioned above, perhaps Arjunavarmadeva wants to contextualize the poem within the setting of a love quarrel in order to spike it with a tension and a brand of exasperated longing that would not otherwise be present. Again, it is the *vipralambha* aspect of *śṛṅgāra* that is favored, and it is also more keenly felt, more psychologically complex and interesting than its alternative.

The ultimate in exasperation, if we are to follow Arjunavarmadeva's reading, is expressed in verse 102:

She's in the house.
She's at turn after turn.
She's behind me.
She's in front of me.
She's in my bed.
She's on path after path,
and I'm weak from want of her.

O heart,
there is no reality for me
other than she she
she she she she
in the whole of the reeling world.

And philosophers talk about Oneness.

Once again, I responded to this poem in much the same manner as I did to verse 64, with this being the masculine version, perhaps a poem about a sophisticated *nāgarika,* an "urbane" man, who is head over heels in love. But instead of reading it as an expression of fullness and joyful craving tinged with comic irony, Arjunavarmadeva once more frames this verse in a context of abject longing. His headnote reads: "A certain man who is separated from his lover deliberates to himself."[19]

Let us look now for a moment at how certain elements in the poems act as signifiers for some of the psychological tensions that are present in *vipralambha* poetry. The two verses that follow are numbers 57 and 69. Verse 57 is written in the form of a dialogue between a woman and a man, a rather nasty little spat crystallized for all time in *śārdūlavikrīḍita* meter, as only Sanskrit can do. Here is the Sanskrit original:

bāle nātha vimuñca mānini ruṃaṃ roṣān mayā kiṃ kṛtam
khedo 'smāsu na me 'parādhyati bhavān sarve 'parādhā mayi
tat kiṃ rodiṣi gadgadena vacasā kasyāgrato rudyate
nanv etan mama kā tavāsmi dayitā nāsmīty ato rudyate

Here is my translation:

My girl.
  Yes, lord?
Get rid of your anger, proud one.
  What have I done out of anger?
This is tiresome to me.
  You haven't offended me.
  All offenses are mine.
So why are you crying yourself hoarse?
  In front of whom am I crying?

In front of me.
    So what am I to you?
You're my darling.
    No, I'm not.
    That's why I'm crying.

Metrically speaking, this verse is a work of genius. *Śārdūlavikrīḍita* ("tiger's play") is a meter with nineteen syllables per line, with *yati,* or caesura, after the twelfth syllable. In this verse, *yati* is never violated and, in fact, follows the syntactic units of the dialogue perfectly: *yati* occurs exactly where the natural pauses in speech would occur, and the verse is, therefore, redolent with a natural quality that is rare in much Sanskrit poetry of the classical period.

What is it about this verse, in particular, that makes it an interesting example of *śṛṅgāra* poetry? In other words, where in this verse can the characteristic tension of *vipralambha* be found? The answer can be found in Vemabhūpāla's commentary. Paying special attention to the vocatives that open the verse, he makes a solid and perceptive argument for the way in which these two words spark off the confrontation in the poem: "In this case, the *nāyaka* addresses a *pragalbhā-nāyikā* (a bold, mature woman) as *bālā,* 'young girl,' by means of *vakrokti* (literally, "crooked speech," a rhetorical figure which consists of an indirect phrase used in some evasive and clever way, often achieved through punning or by employing a certain tone of voice). Thereupon, realizing this, the *nāyikā,* by means of the exact same sort of *vakrokti,* addresses her lover as *nātha,* 'lord,' 'master,' etc." In other words, the man addresses the woman in a manner that suits neither her character nor her experience, and he is therefore making fun of her. The woman realizes that he is being condescending and follows suit by addressing him sarcastically as *nātha,* thereby answering him with *vakrokti,* so the vocatives are tit for tat. The tension is thus immediately established in the first two words of the verse, and it serves to drive a wedge between the male and female characters.

The fissure between them is widened in the phrase that follows, for it is clear that the man understands what the woman means. He then speaks to her directly, asking her to give up her anger. He is now shifted to the position of trying desperately to mollify her, but she continues to answer him with *vakrokti* phrases. The emotion of the poem lies in all of her replies, here posing an interesting semiotic problem.

Words and phrases are suddenly signifying their opposites, and the world of meaning in the poem is turned on its head until the whole situation dissolves, unresolved, into tears at the end of the verse.

But the tension is created not only by the *vakrokti* in the *nāyikā's* replies. It is evident in even more subtle ways in the verse. There is a constant push and pull in the use of pronouns and terms of address in the remaining three lines, as well. The second line begins with *khedo 'smāsu,* literally, "there is pain in us, this troubles us, bothers us, etc." By the use of the "royal we" *(asmāsu),* the man is distancing himself from the woman. She responds to this in kind, in the polite third person, saying, *na me 'parādhyati bhavān;* literally, "Sir has not offended me." She thus maintains the distance that he himself had established, and with *vakrokti* to boot, for *of course* he has offended her, and she means exactly the opposite of what she is actually saying.

In the second verse, number 69, all these issues are truly borne out:

tathābhūd asmākaṃ prathamam avibhaktā tanur iyaṃ
tato' na tvaṃ preyān aham api hatāśā priyatamā
idānīṃ nāthas tvaṃ vayam api kalatraṃ kiṃ aparaṃ
mayāptaṃ prāṇānaṃ kuliśakaṭhinānaṃ phalam idam

My translation:

At first,
our bodies were as one.

Then you were unloving,
but I still played the wretched favorite.

Now you're the master
and we're the wife.

What's next?

This is the fruit I reap
from my diamond-hard life.

Obviously, this verse is the lament of an angry woman to her husband, who is now devoid of love for her. The verse traces the painful dissolution of their relationship and its movement from bliss to bitterness and, simultaneously, from premarital passion to married indifference. The language of this poem is shot through with tension on all sorts of levels. The most obvious, perhaps, is the temporal framework within which this poem is cast. The first three lines begin with phrases that denote sequential time: *Tathābūd . . . prathamam* ("So it was . . . at first"), followed by *tataḥ* ("then . . ."); then *idānīm* ("now . . ."). The future lies at the end of the third line, in the *nāyikā's* question, *kiṃ aparam*? ("What's next?").

Each of these four temporal phrases is followed by the *nāyikā's* characterization of her relationship with her husband in the past, present, and future. The use of number in nouns and pronouns is very telling, and both commentators, Arjunavarmadeva and Vemabhūpāla, also make much of this phenomenon. Let us consider the first line: *tathābhūd asmākaṃ prathamam avibhaktā tanur iyaṃ.* The literal meaning of the words can really tell us a lot. Note, first of all, the plural first-person pronoun *asmākam* ("our") and the way in which it modifies a singular noun and its modifiers, *avibhaktā tanur iyam,* literally, "this body of ours (which was) undivided." This perfectly encapsulates the bliss of their original union; the two became as one and, as plural becomes singular, it is beautifully echoed in the very grammar of the line.

In the second line, the tension begins; the One once more becomes Two. The *tanu,* the "body," splits into *tvam* and *aham,* "You" and "I." What is more, the man has become unloving, *na tvaṃ preyān,* but the woman continues to love him, however miserably: *Aham api hatāśā priyatamā* ("but I was still the wretched favorite").

The third line dissolves into bitterness and total inequality in the present "now": *idānīṃ nāthas tvaṃ vayam api kalatram.* The absolute literal meaning of this phrase is, "Now you're the master, and *we* are the wife," returning to the plural first-person pronoun of the first line. The woman thus distances herself from the man. Vemabhūpāla makes a valuable comment regarding the use of the pronoun *vayam*:[20] "In this case, the plural pronoun 'we' is used out of despair. In instances such as despair, poets employ the plural."

The *nāyikā* also goes so far as nearly to defeminize herself with the neuter word for wife, *kalatram. Kalatram* also has other lexical resonances. It means "wife" or "consort," but it also means "the female of any animal," "hip," and "loins," as well as "female genitals." Arjunavarmadeva interprets it like this: "Now, as if I'm a cow, you are my master."[21] The message is clear, in any case. And *kiṃ aparam?* "What is next?" the woman asks. *Mayāptaṃ prāṇānaṃ kuliśakaṭhinānāṃ phalam idam.* "The fruit that I reap from my diamond-hard life."

As we have seen, all these poems either are about rifts, fissures, and absence, or are interpreted as such. While I like to think that these Sanskrit quatrains were composed in pleasure, it appears that pleasure's "victorious rival,"[22] desire, is what has received the primary focus of the commentators. Barthes has written that "desire denotes a 'class notion.' The 'populace' doesn't know desire, only pleasure. . . . So-called 'erotic' books represent not so much the erotic scene as the expectation of it, the preparation for it; its ascent."[23] Desire, then, lies somewhere beyond the text and beyond the body. The interpretations that I have discussed above are what make the later theologically oriented, antiliterary commentaries on the *Amaruśataka* (such as Ravicandra's) and other erotic texts possible (such as Pītāmbara's commentary on the *Gāthāsaptāśatī*), transforming these poems into fair game for the trite exegeses of religious didacts who sever them from the bodily pleasures and urges about which they were ostensibly composed and bestow on them, at the very best, the driest brand of Barthian "epistemic dignity."

My following discussion of the Prākrit *Gāthāsaptaśatī* and its commentators will illustrate this phenomenon more fully and, in certain fascinating instances, demonstrate cases in which contextual ambiguity has permitted *dhvani*-based interpretation to allow meaning to run amok.

5

Reading the Prākrit *Gāthās*

⁘ According to most accounts, the *Gāthāsaptaśatī* is the oldest extant anthology of poetry from South Asia containing our very earliest examples of secular verse.[1] The language of this anthology, Māhārāṣṭrī Prākrit, is classified by linguists as one of the Middle Indo-Aryan languages, all of which (except for Apabhraṃśa) are included under the generic name Prākrit. The Middle Indo-Aryan category includes dialects from inscriptions dating from the third century B.C.E. through the fourth century C.E., as well as certain literary languages.

The term "Prākrit" is derived from the Sanskrit word *prakṛti*, meaning "making at first," "original source," "nature." Prākrit is the "opposite" of Sanskrit (from *saṃskṛta*, meaning "well-made," "refined," "cultured"). The traditional grammarians of the literary Prākrits argue that these languages are all derived from the Sanskrit language as codified by their predecessor, Pāṇini. But contemporary scholars employ the term Prākrit to refer to South Asian vernaculars, as opposed to Sanskrit, the language of so-called court literature and of the educated and priestly classes. If we examine inscriptional evidence, it is clear that the Prākrits are not derivative. Prākrits were used for inscriptions as early as the third century B.C.E., whereas Sanskrit itself was not employed in inscriptions until as late as the first century C.E.

In many ways, poems composed in Māhārāṣṭrī have elegantly codified for us the domestic and erotic lives of people who lived outside the courtly existence that Sanskrit writers had so exhaustively and beautifully described. In what was perhaps a search for a more "natural" means of expression, the composers of Māhārāṣṭrī *gāthās*, themselves sometimes authors of Sanskrit verse in later periods, chose this Prākrit for composition in order to evoke more accurately life outside the Sanskritic sphere. Though the very word "Prākrit" seems to imply a certain closeness to natural speech, Māhārāṣṭrī was just as "artificial" as Sanskrit, but it seems to have served as a substitute for writers who lacked a vernacular for expressing themes and describing situations that may have been deemed inexpressible or indescribable within the bounds of prevailing literary conventions.

According to the Prākrit grammarians, Māhārāṣṭrī is the Prākrit par excellence. The very term "Prākrit" had become to them, in fact, a metonym for Māhārāṣṭrī—when Prākrit was used in their discussions and analyses, it is clear that Māhārāṣṭrī was usually what they meant. It is obvious that literary Prākrits such as Māhārāṣṭrī must have been artificial, as they were different from the spoken languages contemporaneous with them and probably reflect vernaculars from some former time. So, in a sense, the *prakṛti* versus *saṃsṛkṛti,* or "nature versus culture" dichotomy, is not useful when we describe such a language. One could almost say that Māhārāṣṭrī is a *saṃskṛta-prākṛt,* as it is itself a codified poetic language.

The Sanskrit poet Kālidāsa himself used Māhārāṣṭrī in his dramas, perhaps out of some need for dramatic realism, thereby allowing the "commoners"—and women—in his plays to speak a tongue that could adequately represent or suggest their own dialects. As far as we can tell, Kālidāsa was the first author to incorporate Māhārāṣṭrī into a Sanskrit literary work, using it in the verses spoken by female characters in his dramas. His successors followed suit. George Hart has used this linguistic evidence as the basis for dating the *Gāthā-saptaśatī,* placing it somewhere between Aśvaghoṣa and Kālidāsa (i.e., 200–450 C.E.),[2] which is a reasonable date for later accretions, but Hāla probably compiled the "core text" some 150 years earlier.

Literary historians and orientalists seem to have made the general assumption that Prākrit languages and literatures are unsophisticated and vulgar, thereby perpetuating the useless Prākrit versus Sanskrit or "nature" versus "culture" dichotomy. For many scholars, the term "Prākrit" seems to have suggested something that is both linguistically and morally "degenerate." This dichotomy and the literary expectations from Prākrit texts that it appears to raise have led to rather unfortunate misevaluations and even devaluations of this literature, not by the classical Sanskrit critics but, for the most part, by European and American scholars and translators. Lienhard is correct in pointing out that Māhārāṣṭrī Prākrit was a "privileged language" during Hāla's time, and the *gāthās* were written for urbane, aristocratic consumers.[3] In spite of this, the *Gāthāsaptaśatī*'s detractors and supporters alike have described it as derivative, "folkloric,"[4] and sometimes downright immoral. Arthur Berriedale Keith, in his now classic but hopelessly outdated reference work, *Classical Sanskrit Literature,* rightly claims that Māhārāṣṭrī Prākrit is "far from being a true vernacular," but then wrongly argues that the *gāthās* are derived from the study of Sanskrit models.[5] Keith has also demonstrated that the *Gāthāsaptaśatī* had a far-reaching influence on later authors and compilers of verse anthologies and that it even "found imitators in Sanskrit." He continues to flatter the text, but his true pro-Sanskrit prejudices are clear: "Govardhana's twelfth-century anthology, the *Āryāsaptaśatī*, is a collection of erotic verse arranged in alphabetical order. The work is inferior to Hāla's despite the superior beauty of the Sanskrit."[6] More recently, misapprehensions about the nature, language, and purpose of Māhārāṣṭrī *gāthās* have also led to collections of English translations with preposterous titles such as John T. Roberts's 1986 book, *The Homely Touch: Folk Poetry of Old India* (Lexington, Ky.: Mazda).

Formal Structures and the Problem of Meaning

In formal terms, Māhārāṣṭrī *gāthās* are relatively uncomplicated. The meter of the *gāthā* is what is known in Sanskrit prosody as *āryā,* of which sixteen varieties have been documented in Sanskrit itself. This scheme was more extensively elaborated in Prākrit *gāthās,* among which twenty-seven permutations are known to us. Composed in slightly asymmetrical couplets, a *gāthā* consists of thirty *mātrās,* or "syllabic instants," in the first line, which is subdivided into two *pādas* ("feet"). The first *pāda* consists of twelve *mātrās;* the second, of eighteen. The second line has twenty-seven *mātrās* and is also divided into two *pādas;* the first *pāda* of this line also has twelve *mātrās.* The final *pāda* follows with fifteen. In Prākrit versification, the meter is not based on the number of syllables in a line, as is the case in classical Sanskrit prosody, but is based on the total *length* of syllables in a line.

Therefore, when speaking in terms of bare poetic structure, Prākrit *gāthās* lie somewhere between Tamil and Sanskrit poems in formal complexity. Metrically speaking, they are straightforward, and the poems are probably as brief as any verse could possibly be, maintaining syntactic integrity while carrying optimum amounts of semantic "punch." It is this very structural brevity that led the poets who composed in this genre to explore avenues other than those found in more conventional "representational" or "mimetic" techniques for conveying meaning. This led to the development of a complex symbological system that I would term a "poetics of anteriority." The poet was forced by the brief poetic structure to choose words that had a potential plurality of semiotic referents that existed not in the text as it appeared on the page but somewhere outside of it, or "anterior" to it.

Categories of Interpretation

It is due to this very semiotic complexity that Prākrit *gāthās* appear to fall into two broad and distinct interpretive genres. There are many *gāthās* that could be considered, though anachronistically, as members of a "subgenre" of Sanskrit erotic poetry for the sole purpose of interpretation. In other words, they generously allow themselves to be "read backward" off similar poetry in Sanskrit, and they invite interpretation founded on more traditional dramaturgically based Sanskrit criticism. The same standards, ideas, and rhetorical jargon can easily be applied to the *gāthās* that fall under this category. Here are a few examples, which, for the sake of illustration, I have paired with "twin" Sanskrit poems found in the later *Amaruśataka:*

She scatters
the lotuses of her eyes
up the street,
waiting for you to come,

resting her breasts on the gate
like a pair of auspicious pots.

(*Gāthāsaptaśatī* 2.40)

She made a long garland of welcome
with her eyes alone,
not with blue lotus blossoms.

She scattered the flowers
    with a single smile,
    not with jasmine and such.

She gave the water offering
    with drops of sweat from her full breasts,
    not with water from a pot.

With her own parts alone,
    the slender girl
    bade her entering lover
    auspicious greetings.

(*Amaruśataka* 45)

These two verses employ a similar device, that of the *nāyikā* using her own body to welcome her lover, and not the usual implements of a decorous and more "formal" greeting (i.e., flower petals, sprinklings of water, etc.). Her body and gestures actually become those implements. The only real difference in the above two poems is a temporal one;[7] they offer "before" and "after" descriptions of the same situation and employ the same trope. In the case of the *gāthā,* commentator Mathurānāth Śāstrī offers the following headnote, interpreting the poem as the words of a go-between: "In order to arrange a meeting between the heroine and a hero who was slow in matters of love, a messenger spoke of the intensity of the woman's feelings." This interpretation would be logical and acceptable for a reader who is familiar with the common dramatic contexts that are found in later Sanskrit erotic literature. The *gāthā* allows itself to be "translated" into a Sanskrit interpretive scheme with no trouble at all, and the commentary could just as well have been written by one of the great commentators on the *Amaruśataka.* The jargon and the ideas are indistinguishable. The following pair of poems also illustrates the same principle. Here, in both cases, the poem is spoken by one of the heroine's girlfriends, who is worn out and frustrated by her companion's angry displays. Again, it is easy to see that a Sanskrit critic would have no trouble producing a "dramaturgical" reading of the *gāthā:*

He fell at your feet
    and you ignored him.

He said loving things
    and you spoke without love.
Even when he left,
    you didn't stop him.

So tell me:
    For whose sake
    is all this fuss?

(*Gāthāsaptaśatī* 5.32)

Fickle-hearted girl,
why did you willfully ignore your lover
when he came to your house like that?

He fell at your feet
and was spilling over
with love for you.

So now,
as long as you live,
you'll reject what comes from happiness.

Your comfort's in your crying,
so endure the fruit
of your ill-born, angry acts.

(*Amaruśataka* 56)

We have to be grateful to the later Sanskrit poets who reworked, embellished, and elaborated upon the earlier examples of poetry found in Prākrit that could be described as "representational" or "mimetic" and would thereby appeal to their tastes. Their "reworkings," through the lens of a rhetoric and aesthetics that were based largely on the *Nāṭyaśāstra,* in fact, helped to preserve part of an aesthetic sensibility that was apparently employed by some of the composers of Māhārāṣṭrī *gāthās.* However, in this body of poetry, we find another, larger, and far more difficult symbology at work that appears to have survived "the death of the aesthetics that begat it."[8] As critic Michael Riffaterre writes,

> Conventional poetic forms can be interpreted conventionally so long as the corresponding aesthetics survives. But a reader perceiving them from within another system uses a different her-

> meneutic metalanguage, and in so doing, he still "reacts correctly" to the same language as the original reader did—the text's unchanged language.[9]

In effect, readers are confronted with the problem of trying to make sense out of poetry that is written in a language they know, but a language for which they are unable to construct a coherent "meaning." The poetic vocabulary, in the strict lexical sense, is familiar, but the symbological system is not. This results in interpretive attempts to force poetry that is largely based on a "dead" or no longer accessible system of convention into a "mimetic" frame of reference. In the case of the well-trained Sanskrit reader, a poem such as the one below might only seem like so much "nonsense":

Just today,
  he's gone abroad.
Just today,
  some people are wakeful.
Just today,
  the Godāvarī's banks
  are gold with turmeric.

(*Gāthāsaptaśatī* 1.58)

The questions one might immediately ask are: Who is the speaker? To whom is this poem addressed? Who has gone abroad? Who are these "people" and why are they "wakeful"? Why is the riverbank covered with turmeric? Commentator Mathurānāth Śāstrī has attempted to provide a reasonable context for this poem: "A certain chaste woman, while expounding on the virtues of her much-beloved husband, said this to her mother-in-law to point out the fact that her own bad co-wives were preparing themselves for trysts." The commentary which follows the poem reads:

> "Eager for battle, your son has left home on this very day. And on this very day, because of fear of the approach of thieves, the people who live in the village are very wakeful." This is the meaning that must be supplied. But it is *suggested* that on this very day, the people, that is, my co-wives, are wakeful, too, due to their efforts in preparing for trysts. Today, the banks of the Godāvarī are colored

with turmeric, and the sense here is that, by washing their limbs of the turmeric that was rubbed on them, the bad women are starting to adorn themselves, and so on. The idea is this: Previously, (as long as) your son the village chief is around, the bad wives do not have the temerity to have affairs with other men. Moreover, it is suggested that since this man who is my husband, because he restrains approaching thieves, etc., is valiant, and also that because he enjoys many women, it is all right for him to want sexual relations.

It appears that Mathurānāth Śāstrī generated this somewhat garbled interpretation from the ambiguous phrase "some people are wakeful" and then invented a reasonable, though perhaps forced, interpretation around this "core" of ambiguity. But we must note the plethora of ideas in this commentary. There seems to be no set system of correspondence between "symbol" and "meaning" from which the commentator appears to have worked. Here is another intriguing example:

Those women
who can see their lovers
even in dreams
are lucky.

But without him,
sleep just won't come,
so who can dream
a dream?

(*Gāthāsaptaśatī* 4.97)

At first glance, this little poem seems simple enough, even sentimental and sad, but the commentator Gaṅgādharabhaṭṭa has given this verse an interesting twist by converting it into a boast, and thereby calling my own interpretive instincts into question. His headnote reads: "A woman said this in order to make known the extraordinary nature of her own passion, having been asked by the neighbor-women, 'Why can't you dispel the pain of separation by seeing your lover in a dream?'" The one-line comment that follows the poem reads: "It is suggested that 'In this case, you are the unlucky ones, but I am fortunate.'" In other words, the female speaker is bragging to her friends that the nature of her love relationship is so passionate that she cannot sleep at all and is therefore unable to dream about her lover. The women who can sleep and dream might be lucky, but the speaker is the most fortunate of all because of her constant state of sexual agitation and longing. In this case, Gaṅgadharabhaṭṭa's headnote does not seem to match his one-line commentary, but perhaps that is the point: the poem itself, as it turns out, is ambiguous.

Gāthās such as *Gāthāsaptaśatī* 1.58 appear to "defy" or "resist" meaning outright. Poems such as this—and there are many in the anthology—almost "wink" at us from the page and, at times, seem to dare us to make sense of them. They invite us to participate in a kind of heady interpretive game with them, inciting their readers to generate contexts for them; to "dramatize" them in such a way as to make the poems "cohere" inside the readers' own subjective and known realities. The earliest surviving record of a scholar who rose to meet this interpretive challenge was Ānandavardhana, who composed his *Dhvanyāloka* some seven or eight centuries after the core text of the *Gāthāsaptaśatī* was compiled. I will provide a few examples of his (and to a much lesser extent, Mammaṭa's) illustrative applications of the *gāthās* below.[10]

Inventing Contexts for *Māhārāṣṭrī Gāthās*

In general, readers, commentators, translators, and reviewers are bound to see shadows of themselves or of their own concerns in a poem. A poem is, in fact, a "patch" between desire and reality. Like a dream, a poem can be viewed as "reality encoded."[11] The issue is not what is actually on the page, what critic Harold Bloom calls the "manifest text."[12] The poem is really what exists in that misty place between "writing" and "reading," the "latent text," the poem that lives in symbol or emblem. Though a poem certainly has a static life on a page, the actual events of reading, interpretation, and commentary give a poem a vital historical life. We are fortunate that over a millennium and a half of Sanskrit scholarship has yielded up to us actual records of historical moments of reading. Since these recorded "moments" have become traditionally attached to various types of printed text, many of these commentaries have become as vital as the text itself and, in some instances, have even superseded the text, as is true, I believe, in the case of Abhinavagupta's commentary on Ānandavardhana's *Dhvanyāloka*.

Examples such as this have led many scholars to attach an almost holy sort of significance to Sanskrit commentaries, when, in fact, a great many of them do not warrant reading at all. As in the examples I will cite below, there do exist commentaries that are quite "unholy," ones that we might describe as almost elegant in their perversity.

I had come to expect during the course of my research that I would eventually stumble upon a commentary or perhaps upon a passage in a *śāstra* that would help me crack the rhetorical "code" that would assist me in analyzing some of the more obscure and "defiant" couplets in the *Gāthāsaptaśatī*, such as the ones I have listed above. But what I encountered in the commentaries and *śāstras* was no rhetorical rosetta stone. What I found were not answers but a few suggestions, and I also uncovered some rather interesting agendas. In reviewing all the texts I have surveyed over the past six or seven years, I have come to believe that the agendas of Ānandavardhana and Mammaṭa were honestly rhetorical. Both writers were highly skilled in argument and deeply concerned with the whole semiotic enterprise. Both authors made use of Prākrit couplets in beautifully ingenious ways to discuss the mechanics of *dhvani*. And, sadly, these are the earliest instances of recorded "readings" of Prākrit *gāthās*, meaning that the earliest record of "interpretation" we have for them appears almost eight centuries after the *Gāthāsaptaśatī* was probably compiled.

Ingalls has pointed out that Ānandavardhana and Abhinavagupta were "acquainted with a substantial literature in Prākrit,"[13] and it is this "acquaintance" that strongly suggests that it may have been the challenge—the "defiance" of the Prākrit couplet and its stubborn resistance to more conventional means of interpretation—that inspired Ānandavardhana's formulation of *dhvani* theory. Ingalls has also remarked that Prākrit literature "was an important stimulus to discussion" and that "it is suggestion *(dhvani)* upon which the effect of almost every [Prākrit] stanza depends."[14] Two representative samples of the fascinating ways in which Ānandavardhana and Abhinavagupta have used the Prākrit poems as illustrations of different types of *dhvani,* as well as their subsequent interpretations of the poems (particularly by Abhinavagupta) follow below.

The first and probably the most important of these samples occurs at *Dhvanyāloka* 2.24. Here, Ānandavardhana quotes *Gāthāsaptaśatī* 2.73:

> The hunter's bride,
> her earrings of peacock feathers,
> struts amidst her co-wives,
> their ornaments made
> of elephant pearls.

The above poem is embedded to serve as an illustration in one of Ānandavardhana's larger and more important expositions on the different genres of *dhvani*. By this point in his argument, Ānandavardhana had established two large and overarching genres of *dhvani* at 2.20, *śabdaśaktimūladhvani* ("resonance rooted in the power of a word") and *arthaśaktimūladhvani* ("resonance rooted in the power of meaning"). At *Dhvanyāloka* 2.24, Ānandavardhana subdivides *arthaśaktimūladhvani* into two further and utterly fundamental categories. The distinctions that are drawn by Ānandavardhana at this point are essential from the standpoint of a classical critic's ideas concerning the very origins of poetic convention: "A meaning that throws light on another [poetic] circumstance is [also] known to be of two types: that which takes shape merely by means of bold expression, and that which is naturally possible." Ānandavardhana elaborates a little further on these divisions in the gloss that follows the above statement:

> As well, there are two kinds of meaning that can be spoken of as a suggester in the case of resonance to be suggested by means of a form in which it arises from the power of meaning. The first is that [resonance] which takes shape merely by means of a bold expression (either by an expression of the poet himself or of a character constructed by the poet). The second is that [type of resonance] which is naturally possible.

Ānandavardhana continues that "the sort of resonance that is naturally possible can happen appropriately even in the world outside [of poetry; that is, in "reality"]; its existence does not merely develop by means of verbal expression."

Ānandavardhana then inserts the above *gāthā* as an example to illustrate the kind of poetic resonance that can emanate from an event that could actually exist in reality and does not at all owe its existence to discernible ornaments of poetic expression. In the *Locana* commentary that follows, Abhinavagupta, elaborating on Ānandavardhana's own commentary on this poem at 3.1, provides one of the most fascinating (and probably standard-setting) interpretations of a Prākrit *gāthā* that I have found in this type of literature:

> Attached to *her*, he can kill only a peacock, but [when] attached to the other women, he slaughtered even elephants. This is the way in which the expression conveys her [the bride's] loveliness. By saying that the ornaments of those women are arranged in various ways, and that, due to the arising of disinterest in sex, their chief skill is in the fabrication of arrangements of them [that is, their ornaments], their extreme ill luck in love at the present time is highlighted. In this case, there should not be a doubt that the word "proud" indicates the true meaning of the poet, but has simply come about due to the heroine's lack of judgment due to factors such as her youth. Whether described, or, casting aside description, even if one sees it before one's very eyes in the outside world, then, in either case, this meaning highlights the fabulous beauty of the hunter's wife.

In other words, the young wife is favored by her hunter-husband, even though her co-wives wear ornaments that are made with materials of far greater value. Ānandavardhana and other later commentators suggest that the young wife is so sexually attractive to her husband that he does not have any energy left over for the effort it would take to slaughter elephants to get the pearls from their frontal lobes—all he can manage to kill is a peacock. All subsequent commentators defer to Abhinavagupta on the matter of interpreting this verse. It seems likely to me that it may be this very passage in the *Locana* that has given later rhetoricians and commentators "permission," in a sense, to be more free (for better or worse) in their interpretations of poetry for which *dhvani* seems applicable as a critical principle. This has resulted in a fair amount of commentatorial "play" in later texts. By following Abhinavagupta's lead, subsequent commentators, as we shall see below, have devised their own agendas and "methodologies" for interpreting these enigmatic little couplets.

The commentaries on the *Gāthāsaptaśatī* that followed the

rhetorical *śāstras* were written between the fourteenth (Bhūvanapāla, Vemabhūpāla) and the twentieth centuries (Mathurānāth Śāstrī). I have chosen the latter and the commentary of Gaṅgādharabhaṭṭa (sixteenth century). I find Gaṅgādharabhaṭṭa's commentary on the *gāthās* to be of primary interest, mainly because he does not sidestep the eroticism in the poems. In fact, if anything, he has erred in the opposite direction, and claims that every single couplet in the *Gāthāsaptaśatī* has an erotic meaning, underscoring in a stunning way the dangers of a search for an inherent "homogeneity" in an anthological text such as this. As Riffaterre writes, "The minute sex is mentioned in an obscure text, we set to work decoding every point of obscurity, hoping for erotic innuendos,"[15] and this is precisely what Gaṅgādharabhaṭṭa has done. Divining the essence of some of this commentator's interpretations is, at times, very problematic. I once asked one of my teachers in Madras what reading a *dhvani* poem should be like. He told me, agreeing with Ānandavardhana and others, that *dhvani* should be instantly perceived; that the steps in cognition of a poem's meaning should not even be recognized, even though they are most definitely there. He used the analogy of taking a stack of lotus petals and piercing it with a needle. Though we might recognize later on that each individual petal has been pierced, we do not contemplate it at all while performing the actual act, as each separate piercing of each individual petal represents a step in cognition.[16]

The only authorities Gaṅgādharabhaṭṭa cites are the usual lexica or *koṣas* (especially *Amara* and *Medinī*) and, vaguely, erotic treatises without specifying which ones in particular, though Dundas has managed to hunt down certain citations in Kokkoka's *Ratirahasya*. Gaṅgādharabhaṭṭa makes no mention at all of Ānandavardhana or Mammaṭa, though he has couched his interpretation in the usual jargon of the classical Sanskrit critics and does slip in an unacknowledged quote or two.

But what might have led Gaṅgādharabhaṭṭa to interpret every couplet as a conveyor of erotic meaning? I suggest that the answer lies in the *Gāthāsaptaśatī* itself. Verse 1.2 states:

> Those who don't know how to read
> or listen to Prākrit verse—

when considering Love's realities,
how can they not feel shame?

The verse does not necessarily spell out an underlying purpose for the anthology, but the headnote that Gaṅgādharabhaṭṭa has provided for it is revealing. It reads: *"Gāthā-koṣa-viracana-prayojanam-āha"*; "[The poet] states the purpose of the compilation of this *gāthā* treasury." So, it is apparent that Gaṅgādharabhaṭṭa believed that poetry had a *prayojanam*, a "use," and that in the case of this particular text, its "use" was to educate a person about love. And so, this must have been the assumption under which he was laboring, and with stunning results.

Let us consider for a moment the most quoted verse from the collection, 1.4:

Look,
a still, quiet crane
shines on a lotus leaf
like a conch shell lying
on a flawless emerald plate.

We are to understand that the vivid simile in this verse is part of a larger scenario: a woman and her lover are walking along a riverbank and she spots a crane. She describes for the man a tranquil scene with an artful, well-matched simile. At first glance, the inclination would be to read this verse as a descriptive one and nothing more, but in the *Kāvyaprakāśa*, Mammaṭa cites it as an example of *dhvani* at 2.7: "Here, by [the crane's] quietude, a state of confidence [is suggested], and by that [state of confidence], that the place is devoid of people. So, some woman indicates to some man that the spot is suitable for trysting." Mammaṭa continues: "Or, [the meaning] 'you're lying, you didn't show up for our tryst' is suggested." In other words, Mammaṭa has read this verse to suggest that the woman is trying to seduce the man, or she is accusing him of having missed an earlier rendezvous in that very spot. The place is a good one for a secret meeting. This is indicated by the stillness of the crane—if people were around, the bird would probably have flown away.

But here is Gaṅgādharabhaṭṭa's utterly remarkable interpretation. The headnote that he has provided reads:

> One's train of thought can be fixed on places such as rivers, forests, and caves, or on places which are hard to reach. Beginning with gentle steps, a man whose calm is unbroken can revel in sexual pleasures for quite a while, even though he is tired. Such things are found in the love treatises, and in this poem, a certain woman says this (to a man), making his mind focus on something else, so that they can have intercourse for a longer time.

The commentary that follows puts these words in the woman's mouth: "If you are opposed to checking your speed, then look at that crane, and fix your mind on something else so that you can make love to me for a longer time." (The erotic treatises call this *anyacittatā*, "putting one's thoughts on other things.")

One naturally wonders what it was about this poem that gave Gaṅgādharabhaṭṭa such an idea, but as we read on in the text, we encounter more *gāthās* for which he has offered similar interpretations. There are two more or less common elements in the poems. First, they are all poems of natural description. Second, most of them begin with the imperative command, "Look!" Here are three more examples:

Look,
  a spider clings
  by its upturned legs
  to its own silk,
  hanging from the thatch
  like a lone bakula blossom
  strung on gossamer thread.

(1.63)

Look,
  rubies and emeralds mixed
  fall from heaven
  like a necklace unstrung
  from the throat of the sky goddess:
A line of parrots.

(1.75)

With the cooing of pigeons
nesting on roof pegs

that you can barely see,
the temple moans in pain
as if pierced by a spike.

(1.64)

Gaṅgādharabhaṭṭa's readings of these poems present us with an extremely interesting paradox. There is no sex in these *gāthās* per se (i.e., on the page as "manifest text"), but they become perhaps the only verses in *all* of classical Indian love lyric in which the poem is situated *in flagrante delicto,* if we decide to accept Gaṅgādharabhaṭṭa's interpretation. It seems here that everything is in the gaze, not in the Lacanian sense but in an almost tantric, meditative sense. The sex act seems to be contained in a nonverbal, supratextual anterior "gesture" that hovers in a place somewhere off the page: it lives in the "latent text." Other poems are certainly about the act itself, but the interesting thing to note is that these other poems are always about past or future sex, never about "present-tense" intercourse. And, if we follow this line of interpretation, "present-tense" intercourse only happens in poems in which there *is* no intercourse depicted in the poem on the actual page!

In Gaṅgādharabhaṭṭa's case, these poems needed to be assigned a "use," a *prayojanam,* and an erotic one at that, perhaps out of a need for homogeny or for, perhaps, a sort of Aristotelian need for "organicity" or "congruence" in the text. Randomness makes commentators, philologists, and textual formalists very nervous. Poems cannot be "about what they are about." The minute poems are written, they are shoved into history, and their authors are never again in possession of their own intended meanings. Commentaries do, however, preserve for us readings of prevailing cultural paradigms into poems.

Generally speaking, in the later commentaries we can note that, at times, the tone of argument no longer seems to be concerned with issues of textual interpretation or of the production of meaning. Instead, the discourse takes a much more personal and private turn. One gets the sense when reading sections of Mathurānāth Śāstrī's 1933 commentary, for instance, that he was a harried householder who was preoccupied with his own domestic situation, however exhaustive, thorough and faithful to his own stated agenda (that every single word in the *Gāthāsaptaśatī* can be shown to emit *dhvani*) he may have been. As one can hear strains of domestic violence and the music of polka bands wafting up from the street in several of Mahler's symphonies, one can also hear obbligatos of disputes with his wife and problems with his children in the India of the 1930s in Mathurānāth Śāstrī's commentary. His own interpretation often crops up at the end of his encyclopedic lists of quotes from the usual literary *śāstras* and other commentaries, and, more often than not, it says something like: "This *gāthā* was repeated to a younger woman to teach her that she should not shirk her domestic duties . . . *iti dhvanyate*."[17]

On the other hand, Gaṅgādharabhaṭṭa wants everything to be "erotic," but there is a darker side to his commentary than I have thus far made apparent. For the sake of illustration, let us briefly look at a poem from the Sanskrit *Subhāṣitaratnakoṣa* and at what Mammaṭa had to say about it, and then compare it with a thematically similar Prākrit *gāthā* and at what sort of context Gaṅgādharabhaṭṭa has provided for it.

The first verse is a Sanskrit poem attributed to a poet with a woman's name, or possibly by an actual female poet, Sīlābhaṭṭārikā, about whom nothing is known:

> That man, thief of my innocence,
> he's none other than my husband.
> These are the same spring nights,
> and these fragrant breezes
> are still laden with the scent of opened jasmine.
>
> And that girl, she's me.
> But there—the dalliance and lovemaking
> on the banks of the Revā
> on the ground beneath the cane trees—
> that's what my heart wants.

Mammaṭa cites this poem in the first chapter of his *Kāvyaprakāśa* as an example of a poem that is *rasavat* ("*rasa*-infused") and lacking in ornamentation. Mammaṭa is very nonjudgmental, even reverent, about the poems he cites and very simply says about this one: "In some instances, even when there is an obvious absence of ornament, there is no lessening of poeticality." The Prākrit *gāthā* reads:

> I'm telling the truth.
>
> I'm standing at death's door
> and even today,
> my sight falls
> on that thicket
> on the Tāptī's pure banks,
> just as it used to.
>
> (3.39)

Gaṅgādharabhaṭṭa's headnote reads: "A woman said this in order to instruct a male relative that women should never be trusted."

In conclusion, I would like to reiterate the fact that the authors of the literary treatises wanted to demonstrate *how* poems meant, whereas these commentators were more interested in *what* poems meant and, further, in what they could be *used* for. Unfortunately, I have really only hinted at the rather drastic shift in register that occurs in what we take for later literary discourse in Sanskrit, but as contemporary scholars begin to take the art and artifice of the Sanskrit literary commentary more seriously as a means to chart trends in South Asian intellectual and aesthetic history, our general view of developments in South Asian literature will be far more meaningful, nuanced, and complete.

6

Conclusion

In contemplating the interpretive foci and critical methods for these three literary establishments, I have come to several conclusions. In my opening pages, I addressed the problem of attempting to arrive at a definition of what we might term a "Pan-Indian classical love lyric." On the level of fundamental materials—that is, the building blocks in South Asian intellectual, emotional, and geophysical environments that provide the necessary "gestalts" from which poetic conventions are built—we can speak of "commonalities." On this very basic level—the level of the "pre-text"—there are indications that reflexively lead us to search for many common threads, for it quite naturally follows that many of the poetic conventions that we find in Old Tamil, Sanskrit, and Māhārāṣṭrī Prākrit verse appear to be the same: they have been formulated, in many instances, from the same environmental gestalts. However, we can only arrive at a unified definition if we choose to leave these poems somehow denuded, that is, if we peel away issues of authorial nuance, questions of aesthetic response, and the issues surrounding the identities of intelligent readers. If we choose, as did I. A. Richards and other past and present adherents to the school of New Criticism, to read poetry only as "text," as an authorless, readerless entity without history or potential pluralities of meaning, then, yes, a monolithic definition of what a love poem *is* in the South Asian classical context can easily be devised.

But I hope that I have made it quite clear from the evidence that I have presented above that these poems and the systems devised for reading them are inextricably linked. Because of its very nature, "reading" is an act that destabilizes meaning, no matter how "fixed" or "rigid" a system of interpretation might be—there is no one "right way" to read a poem in any of these traditions. These poems, especially the Māhārāṣṭrī couplets, are like molecules with unstable outer valences. They move through history, various critics and commentators attach meaning to them, and by the time we find ourselves grappling with the act of interpretation in the present—in a current historical "moment" of reading—we find ourselves contending not just with a denuded, ahistorical poem, but with a poem with polyvalent clusters of meaning attached to it, still unstable, still requiring a response from us. So again, even if the conventions in all three traditions were identical, if the "signifiers" were indistinguishable, the ideas and the "culture" that they signify are naturally bound to have many shades and degrees of difference.

I have also demonstrated above that the act of "reading" in the Sanskrit and Tamil traditions are quite different intellectual and aesthetic processes, and the ways in which Sanskrit and Tamil rhetorical traditions have developed "taxonomies" for the human love experience are also vastly different. Due to this difference in "love taxonomy," the sexual cultures that are reflected by the erotic anthologies are also markedly different, and, in many ways, these final pages represent a tentative and preliminary articulation of this problem. I do not at all pretend that these poems are "historical texts" in the strict sense, nor do I read them as such. Writing on the epic poem the *Rāmāyaṇa,* historian Romila Thapar states:

> Poems as literary forms, even if they should be dealing with historical themes, cannot in themselves be regarded as historical texts. They can at best provide clues to the ways in which people perceived the past or their own times. Such clues are important to the historical reconstruction of ideologies and attitudes, but are not evidence of historical events unless proven to be so from other contemporary historical sources.[1]

I basically agree with Thapar's position and would add that, although the poems which I analyze below do not reflect hard historical reality, they can be read as "cultural metaphors"[2] and are expressed in very specific "cultural idioms."[3] Though aestheticized, the poems represent aspects of romantic and sexual culture, and I assert that we can read them as indices of specific cultural attitudes toward the erotic.

What can these poems tell us about women and men? What kinds of interpersonal dynamics do they represent? These questions have led me to reformulate many of the issues surrounding cultural representations of gender and sexuality in the classical poems, accepting, as I do, that although these works are not hard history, neither are they ahistorical floating manuscripts composed of mere jumbles of metaphor and tangled limbs. They do provide us with evidence of "social practice" manifested in metaphor and idiom.

Two factors predominate—space and sexuality. First, I will discuss aspects of space in these poems, how the authors have circumscribed it and then used it as an arena for the movements and trajectories of their characters. I will be paying particular attention to the portrayal of the characters, and how their physical environments confine and limit them. I will then turn to the representation of sexual relations themselves, and how these relations are encoded in the poems to construct different grammars of love.

Space, Movement, and Feminine Sexuality

One thing that is apparent in Tamil poetry is that physical movement is absolutely free from context to context. Men and women can come and go inside the poetic microcosm. Men may move freely from *akam* ("interior") spaces to *puṟam* ("exterior") spaces, and from context to context. Women may also move freely among the *akam* contexts, but it is only the mother who may cross the membranous boundary between *akam* and *puṟam*. As I stated in the introduction, parents are fully fleshed characters in *cañkam* poetry, and this fact sets the *cañkam* tradition quite apart from the world of Sanskrit convention. For instance, we hear the mother's voice most clearly in the *pālai* context, as in *Naṟṟiṇai* 110.[4] The mother—here, the *naṟṟāy*, or biological mother of the girl, speaks. She can be portrayed as being comforted by the *cevili-t-tāy*, the girl's foster mother, in other contexts such as *mullai*, but we only hear her actual voice, it seems, in the harsh language of *pālai-t-tiṇai*. The *Aiñkuṟunūṟu* contains a decad of *pālai* poems titled *makaṭ-pōkkiya vaḻi-t-tāy irañku pattu*, "the decad of the mother's lamentations at the elopement of her daughter." Translations of several of these poems follow below in chapter 14.

We also hear the *naṟṟāy's* voice in the *puṟam* context of *vākai*, also the name of a flower, but usually translated as "victory." It is interesting within the context of gender roles and their construction in *cañkam* imagery that this is the *puṟam* category that is analagous to *akam's pālai*. The cursing of and grieving over the daughter is transformed into vain and bitter praise for the son in this parallel context. Many of the *vākai* poems describe a son's valor on the field of war. They also wrenchingly reflect the *naṟṟāy's* wish to see her son return home once more, but perhaps the most stunning parallels between the *tiṇai* divisions of *akam* and *puṟam* lie in the relationship between *neytal*, the *tiṇai* of jilted women who lament when their lovers leave them, and the *tiṇai* called *tumpai*, that of "battle frenzy," in *puṟam* situations, wherein the salty pools of tears and marshy, unfirm land in the romantic contexts are transformed into the pools of blood and the gore-soaked battlefields of war.

In the world of *cañkam* imagery, the whole land itself is involved in romance and sex, and is allowed to emote. But there are also poems in the *cañkam* anthologies in which the land is metaphorically allowed to kill. Some poems describe love as an utterly obliterative and destructive force. In fact, the three most common Tamil terms for love, *kāmam*, *iṉpam*, and *aṉpu*, are all derived from negative verbal roots. *Iṉpam* and *aṉpu* are respectively derived from the negative roots *il* and *al*, both of which mean "not to be." The word *kāmam* also appears very early on in Tamil literature. Traditional Tamil linguists derive it from *kātu*, a root meaning "to kill, slay, or obliterate," even though it is obviously identical with the Sanskrit word for desire, *kāma*.

When we shift into the Prākrit poetic microcosm, what immediately stands out is the fact that the world that is circumscribed by these poets suddenly becomes much smaller, in contrast to the vast, teeming emotional landscapes of the Tamil *cañkam* world. The focus is more domestic (although the Tamil world also includes poems focused inside homes and kitchens). Possible settings in the Prākrit world include riverbanks, kitchens, yards, rice fields, hemp fields, and even burning grounds. But unlike Tamil poetry, a Prākrit poem never refers to worlds or arenas of discourse outside of itself. Even though men and women still have the same freedom to move inside and outside the bounds of the home, and even of the village (which is, by and large, the locus for these poems), men do most of the moving, and it is only the *asatī*, or "bad woman," who has much freedom to move anywhere. Here is a poem in the form of a curse (many of the poems in the *Gāhāsaptaśatī* take on this form, and are funny, ironic, and often peppered with threats of sexual impotence and name-calling). It is an oath uttered by a woman whose rival has left for the next village (the headnote of the commentator Gaṅgādharabhaṭṭa reads, "Seeing the many lovers who had started out after a bad woman who had gone to live in another village, some woman said this in jest"):

> Gone to another village
> and luring a pack of dogs,
> may she live with unbroken good fortune
> for a hundred years,
> that bitch of mine.
>
> (*Gāthāsaptaśatī* 7.87)

The encoding of suggestion here is fairly obvious. The "dogs" refer to a line of men who are panting after the woman, the "bitch in heat." *Asatīs* can go off and live by themselves in other villages, but the *satīs*, the "good wives," stay back, and, as the commentator Bhūvanapāla has suggested, the woman who is saying this is hoping that happiness will return to her own house after the *asatī* leaves.

If we return briefly to the pair of poems I introduced in the introductory section (*Gāthāsaptaśatī* 2.68 and *Amaruśataka* 100), it is striking that there seems to have been a movement away from the field and village into town when we enter the Sanskrit poetic locus. The circle is also drawn more tightly around the woman; the suitor moves from "the borders of the fields on the borders of her village" to "roaming the streets near her house"; from fields to streets and from village to town. By the time we enter the world of Sanskrit poetry, the woman has become completely confined to the indoors, unless she tries to slip out for a tryst in her role as *abhisārikā*. And, if we carefully examine the poems of the *Amaruśataka*, we find that she rarely ever makes it. In the Sanskrit world, sex is largely confined to the boudoir, shut away in a room. Love becomes an experience confined to two. Children are replaced by caged bedroom parrots and parents are often referred to as *gurus* and rarely by their relational names. In fact, the whole world of the Sanskrit heroine becomes one of isolation from her own family, and very nonrelational. We can never be certain from the language in the poems, except for a few stray exceptions, that she even has the appellation of "bride." The only relationship the woman is allowed to have with anyone other than the man is with her group of girlfriends, her *sakhīs*, whose only function is to incite her to acts of jealousy to get the man to pay attention to her.

This underscores the striking movement away from public and individual aspects of what I can only call "sexuality" into a more private and yet oddly depersonalized realm. The word "sexuality" connotes the behaviors represented in these poems in the same way that David Halperin[5] has chosen to use it, that is, in a very qualified way. Sexuality can only be defined with what we know of ourselves and how our own cultures construct it. The "sexuality" of an ancient culture can only be thought of as sexual behavior that existed well before our contemporary notions of what constitutes sexuality even existed. These poems are artistic representations of what sexuality in classical India *might have been*, and these representations are not of female sexuality per se, but representations of male attempts to aesthetically capture and portray female sexuality. I would like to trace the movement of classical sexuality as represented in these poems, from the public domain to the private, and to suggest what ramifications they have for trying to recover a "feminine."

There are a great many Tamil poems that incorporate descriptions of wild public displays of lust, anger, and frustration. The best known among these would be the verses composed in *kai-k-kiḷai-t-tiṇai*, the genre of one-sided, unreciprocated love, in which there is the convention called *maṭal*. In *maṭal*, the male characters are the ones who lose control of themselves, mounting horses made of palmyra stems and galloping up and down the town streets, proclaiming their lovesickness to all and sundry, to anyone who will listen. But the exchanges we find depicted in some of the poems of *Naṟṟiṇai* represent not only male-female tensions but also tensions among socioeconomic classes.[6] The frankness of expression in the language of these poems is fairly startling when compared to the sexual semantics of the Prākrit *gāthās* and the Sanskrit love lyrics of the Amaru collection.

Prākrit *gāthās*, which are perhaps from a slightly earlier time period than the Tamil poems, also come from a different, more heavily "Sanskritized" geographic area. Public brawling over sexual matters is a popular theme in the poems, but the language of indirect expression is favored as the medium in poetic representations of these types of situations, as exemplified in the following two poems from the *Gāthāsaptaśatī*. Each *gāthā* represents a similar public situation in which a sexual insult is hurled. The first *gāthā* is spoken by one woman to another; the second by a woman to a molasses maker. I will present each poem with headnotes provided by the sixteenth-century commentator on the text, Gaṅgādharabhaṭṭa:

> *Addressed by a neighbor thus, "You are a slut," a woman replied:*
>
> Okay, so I'm bad.
> Go away, faithful wife.
> Your name may be untarnished,
>
> but at least we don't
> lust after the barber
> like somebody's wife we know.
>
> (*Gāthāsaptaśatī* 5.17)

Gaṅgādharabhaṭṭa's brief commentary beautifully highlights the topsy-turvy nature of the Prākrit insult: Yes means no; good means bad. He writes, "*Pativrate* (this term literally means 'one whose vow is her husband') is a censorious address here. 'Like somebody's wife' means 'you, yourself.' The idea is, 'I may be a slut, but I'm attached to a high type of man. But you are attached to a barber. Your *gotra* ('name') hasn't been tarnished but your *kulam* ('family') certainly has been."

The second poem with its headnote reads:

Making her passion apparent by means of a double entendre, a loose woman spoke of crushing sugar cane to a molasses maker:

Mechanic,
  you're trying to make molasses
  but you're not using the machine
  the way I want you to.

Stupid,
  don't you know
  that you can't make molasses
  without juice?

(*Gāthāsaptaśatī* 6.54)

I need not quote anything from the commentary here, since the overtones are obvious, and what I infer from this poem for once matches Gaṅgādharabhaṭṭa's interpretation exactly. In the poems of the *Gāthāsaptaśatī*, women are often portrayed as sexually hungry, and, although their interchanges are still played out in "public space," the language used becomes more veiled and oblique, even when women are speaking to one another. They are portrayed as having just as many choices as do female characters in Tamil poetry. They can speak as mothers or as daughters; as married or single; as sisters, mistresses, girlfriends, courtesans, or bawds. But their language slips under a cloak of indirection, which may indicate the beginning of a shift from a public sexuality into one that is esoteric, privatized, cloistered, and defused.

By the time we move into the world of Sanskrit poetry, the options for women that I have listed above are greatly rewritten and restructured. Women's speech, gestures, and roles become frozen in those accepted by the Sanskrit stage. The "feminine" is moved indoors, largely trapped inside the house, and fossilized into the different stock roles articulated in the categories of *nāyikā*. Some examples of the types of Sanskrit heroine include the woman whose husband is abroad, the one who has adorned herself and is waiting for her lover to come to her, and the *abhisārikā,* the woman who leaves the house for a secret tryst with her lover, which is rarely actually consummated. In other words, the woman's role is always relative to the actions of the man. In this sequestered world, the woman is treated as something to be studied, typified, measured, and endlessly described.

In Search of Masculine Sexuality

My search for poetic representations of masculine sexuality led me to another anthology of erotic verse in the Prākrit corpus, and I have chosen to analyze certain sections of the *Vajjālagga*, "The Composition Characterized by Topical Sections," another somewhat later anthology of Māhārāṣṭrī Prākrit couplets.[7] The text is undated, but Warder,[8] Lienhard,[9] and others place its compilation at some point in the mid- to late-eighth century C.E., at a time when Prākrit compositions were giving way to works in Apabhraṃśa. This is evident in the text, which, although composed in Jaina Māhārāṣṭrī, demonstrates a strong Apabhraṃśa influence. The poems are ascriptionless and were most likely composed between the second and eighth centuries. The text as we now have it consists of 789 couplets, 82 of which are also found in the earlier *Gāthāsaptaśatī*.

There are two major commentaries available. There is one anonymous commentary and one by Ratnadeva, whose date is reported as 1337 in one manuscript and 1496 in another.[10] In his Sanskrit commentary on the first *gāthā* of this anthology, he characterizes the text and its compiler thus: "The poet named Jayavallabha, crest-jewel of the Śvetāmbara sect, noticing that people were interested in love but dim when it came to Sanskrit, made this collection of Prākrit *gāthās,0* though himself fully conversant in Sanskrit."

The *Vajjālagga* is further characterized by Warder as containing "peculiarities," verses about "machinery" couched in a "technical language that is suggestive of sexual intercourse" but in actuality "has very little to say about sex" except to describe it as "mechanical and laborious," prescribing that the "man should hold back to enable the woman to obtain full satisfaction."[11] M. V. Patwardhan declares that *vrajyās* 50–56 and 61 are "full of obscene thoughts" and that these eight sections form the "pornographic core of the entire collection."[12] One cannot fail to note here that the *vrajyās* characterized by Patwardhan as "obscene" and "pornographic" are the ones that are on men, save for section 50, which contains twenty-five verses on *asatīs,* or "bad women." But this section contains verses that are no more graphic than other verses in the collection—in fact, they border on the conventional. There are verses in other sections that contain unusually graphic descriptions of vulvas, as well as the endless and more common descriptions of female breasts, thighs, and buttocks, but these escape Patwardhan's condemnations.

These "obscene" sections bear titles that range from the benign to the utterly blatant. There are *vrajyās* devoted to *jyautiṣikas, lekhakas, vaidyas, dhārmikas, yāntrikas, musalas,* and *kūpakhanakas*—astrologers, writers, doctors, pious men, mechanics, pestles, and well diggers. But the poems themselves disclose a kind of metaphorical code that is somewhere outside of what I have presently come to understand to be the poetics of sexuality in early South Asian poetry. I can only describe this "coding" as the Prākrit brand of sexual "slang," interesting in that it provides us with a record of a Middle Indo-Aryan sexual "idiolect," rather that what I would term a true "poetics." Here are four examples, two each from the *jyautiṣika*- and *lekhaka-vrajyās:*

497. The astrologer,
    a long piece of chalk in his hand,
    roams in the middle of town.
He knows the movements of Venus
    and if anyone says "Calculate,"
    he calculates.

498. Astrologer,
    don't waste time.
    Take up your piece of chalk
    and calculate for me, quick.

Though Mars has vanished,
    the movements of Venus
    are just as before.

509. The ink is spattered,
the pen broken,
and the page all spoiled!

Damn you,
clumsy scribe!
Even now,
you thirst to write.

510. The inkwell is deep,
the ink is there,
the page spread out.

Wretched writer,
you've broken your pen
writing for people
like us.

Ratnadeva provides the equivalences, perhaps unnecessarily, in a language that is an odd admixture of frankness and euphemism. For the first set of poems, he glosses *khaṭikā,* "chalk piece," as *śepha,* "penis," and *śukra,* "Venus," as *saptama-dhātu,* "the seventh substance," "semen." He substitutes the verb *yabh,* "to have sex"—the so-called vulgar word for the act and roughly equivalent in register and meaning with the English "to fuck"—for the verb *gaṇ,* "to reckon," "count," "figure out." According to him, the intention of the poem is this: "The astrologer, whose penis is long, roams in the middle of town. He knows how to control his ejaculations. If anyone asks him to have sex with them, he'll perform." Ratnadeva, in a rather unusual turn, then assigns the poem to a first-person and presumably male speaker: "By means of checking my emission, I'll satisfy her to the point of orgasm." This assignation, by the way, is rather outside of the usual Prākrit commentarial pale—I would expect a woman speaker here.

As if they bear repeating, Ratnadeva's equivalences for the second set of poems are *vīrya,* "semen," for *maṣī,* "ink," *śepha,* "penis," for *lekhanī,* "pen," and *śayyāpracchādanapaṭam,* "bedsheet," for *tāla-patram,* "surface of the leaf or page," in the first poem. In the second example, Patwardhan substitutes *varāṅga,* "the part of choice," or "vulva," for "page" in a marginal note, and suggests that *maṣībhājana,* "inkwell," must stand for testicles.[13]

Even though there are poems that treat masculine sexuality with greater delicacy (we encounter a few in the Tamil anthologies and in the *Gāthāsaptaśatī*), they are fairly rare, and the commentators seem to miss the point of these poems. Here is an example from the *Gāthāsaptaśatī*, which is built on the common trope of the man as cultivator and the woman as field:

> I'll make love with her here—
>
> while he thinks this
> with his heart,
> the sowing seed
> wet with sweat
> from the wretch's hand
> drops to the ground.
>
> (*Gāthāsaptaśatī* 4.58)

Commentator Gaṅgādharabhaṭṭa seems to miss the metaphor completely. His headnote states: "'Somatic displays can come about merely from emotion.' Some woman said this to a friend to make her own cleverness known." His commentary that follows the verse uselessly speculates on what type of seed it might have been, and human seed, semen, is not considered as an option!

Why do the four poems that I have cited from the *Vajjālagga* "fail"? And what is it, exactly, that these poets are making an effort to represent? Do they give us a picture of a "lived" sexuality? Do they at all exhibit, in the code of the poetic imaginary, the experience of living in a male body? As Paul Smith writes in his 1988 article titled "Vas," "talking about male sexuality is both difficult and deadly easy,"[14] meaning, perhaps, that the masculine is both nowhere at all and everywhere at once. Smith makes the persuasive argument that "sexuality has chronically been 'feminized,' but the concern is male-centered." Certainly in the classical textual traditions of South Asia, the female body is what undergoes examination and articulation with descriptive systems that are bound in a discourse that might be called "biologic." The female form is subjected to endless taxonomies and dissected to the point of absurdity. In the process, masculinity becomes suppressed and relatively unarticulated. As a result of this, the male symbologies that surface are certainly "somatic in their origins, but are actually imaginarily 'spoken' through particular cultural representations"[15] that are focused on concerns with the feminine. As did Freud, perhaps these male poets "made a strange alliance with the feminine, which was very likely a colonizing alliance,"[16] in their attempts to establish a discourse about themselves.

In effect, we learn two things about men from these poems. We learn about desire, what men think about women, and we also learn about anxiety, what men think women think about men, resulting in poems about spilled ink, broken pens, and functional and dysfunctional chalk pieces.

The most unsubtle of the poems from the *Vajjālagga,* in which the whole idea of suggestive poetry is totally defeated, destroy *vyañgyā,* or suggestion, and set up the symbology in such a way that the *abhidhā,* or literal level of the utterance, becomes itself and not *vyañgyā:* the signifier becomes reflexive and is merely signifying itself: *vyañgyā* collapses into *abhidhā.* This results not in what Roland Barthes would call a "failure of symbolization" but in a masculine symbology that has become wildly dysfunctional. Because male desire and anxiety are all mediated through an obsession with the feminine subject, the "masculine" becomes largely "unsymbolizable." Save for a few very rare and transcendent examples, male poets are adept—or are at least consistent—in their representations of themselves through the construction of women, but they fail rather horribly when it comes to representing or interpreting themselves. Here are two more couplets from the *Vajjālagga,* found in the section titled *musala-vajjā,* or "the section on pestles":

541. Friends,
I've combed the village
a hundred times over

and I've yet to see a pestle
that measures up to the mortar
in my house.

538. In the homes of
fortunate women
are found serviceable pestles,

finely turned, long
and bound with a stout strip.

The Prākrit poems on pestles that we find may seem funny to us because of their utter banality, but this is the kind of metaphor that has left its own type of ominous cultural trace, and modernity has bestowed upon it its own perversions. Metaphors have social lives, and sometimes tend to represent more sinister purposes. The metaphor of the "serviceable pestle" signifies sexual satisfaction but has also been enlisted for more nefarious purposes. The grinding stone has become a popular weapon of mayhem directed at a spouse, for instance, and I cannot resist citing a few lines of a song collected by the gifted anthropologist Margaret Trawick from a Kuravar woman in Tamilnadu. What follows is a section of a hymn to Singamma, a woman who was locked up in a forest house, gang-raped, and then murdered by her own brothers for escaping and going to the market. The effect is chilling:

Leaving you within the house, Singamma,
All four doors they closed and locked and came, Singamma.
All four men went inside the house, Singamma.
And as they went inside the house, Singamma,
the mortar stone pounds, doesn't it, Singamma.
And as the mortar stone pounds, Singamma,
all four doors they pulled shut and locked, Singamma.[17]

In conclusion, I hope that the above examples point to a need for a formal and thorough reevaluation of the ways in which we choose to address ourselves to texts and how cultural "objects" have signifying powers that are well beyond artifactual and philological levels. We must begin to rewrite our own old, careworn scholarly paradigms, and, in order to do so, there must be a requestioning of descriptive and significative systems, themes, mythologies, and, most importantly, the very histories of these semiological dynamics and how they relate to our present realities in our own constant reconfigurations of sexuality, gender, and violence. I invite, challenge, and encourage my readers to forge their own new interpretive scripts as they read through my translations in part 2.

Part Two

TRANSLATIONS

7

Young Women Speak to Their Female Friends

"Like an Image on a Mirror, My Pain Will Not Enter Him"

In the forty poems in this chapter, the speaker is, in every case, an unmarried girl who speaks to her girlfriend or friends about her romantic relationship. Poems 7.1–7.7 depict an array of lovesick heroines—the speakers have fallen madly in love with men whom they have seen or made love to in secret. In the case of poem 7.5, the lovers have missed a previously arranged assignation. The Sanskrit poems and the single Prākrit *gāthā* in this group are classified as poems evoking *vipralambha-śṛṅgāra-rasa,* or the mood of love in separation, whereas all the Tamil poems are set in the *kuṟiñci* context, that of clandestine love in union, highlighting the different ways in which readers have traditionally understood and categorized the pains and pleasures of falling in love in these traditions (see chapter 2 above). Poems 7.8–7.18 are spoken by women who have more mature relationships with their men. They speak with great confidence, enthusiastically praise love itself, and even boast of the deepness of their passion. According to commentator Gaṅgādharabhaṭṭa, poem 7.8 is spoken by a woman "in order to make known the extraordinary nature of her own passion," so we are to understand it as a boast rather than as a sad complaint. Like poem 7.8, poem 7.15 is also a Prākrit *gāthā,* and Gaṅgādharabhaṭṭa understands this highly unusual poem about *satī* in the following way. His headnote reads: "A woman said this in order to illustrate the remarkable passion of women, and that even when the husband has died, her goal is to please the heart of her beloved."

Poems 7.19–7.25 are about love spats in which young women feign anger to manipulate their lovers. Their conceits sometimes backfire in countermanipulation, as illustrated by poems 7.21 and 7.22. The *Amaruśataka* provides the finest examples of this theme. Poems 7.26 and 7.27, both Prākrit *gāthās,* are spoken by experienced, witty heroines. The speaker in poem 7.26 comments to a friend on the destruction of a favorite trysting spot, and poem 7.27 is aimed at a rival who has been caught leering coquettishly at the speaker's man. The two Sanskrit poems that follow are beautiful examples of a suspicious heroine confronting a trusted go-between who comes back from the man bearing marks of having had intercourse with him herself. Poems 7.30–7.40 are spoken by heroines, smarting from their experiences but much wiser, on being jilted and on the fickle nature of men in general. Poem 7.35, a Prākrit *gāthā,* is spoken by a woman who complains that her lover only wants her when he cannot have her while she is menstruating—which is indicated by the reference to the "*ghī* and pigment" that she had smeared on her face.

7.1

Forget about trusting in friends.

Because I'm shy,
I can't even pierce that man
who knows my innermost desires
with a well-placed glance

and these local types
are good at poking fun—
they divine
even the subtlest of hints.

I've had it, Mother.
Where do I go for help?

The fire of love
is dying out in my heart.

(*Amaruśataka* 63, Sanskrit)

7.2

Because wretches
will dash a club
against a pinprick,

even though we live
in the same village,
I can't even look at my lover
with both eyes at once.

(*Gāthāsaptaśatī* 6.1, Prākrit)

7.3

Sister,
they gang together in a line
like a bunch of mountain goddesses
and don't fail to stare at me
wherever I go,
saying, "Good girl! Good girl!"
So tell me why I'm no good
to that lord of the mountain.

(*Aiñkuṟunūṟu* 204, Tamil)

7.4

A seated cripple
sees a comb of honey
on a tall hill covered
with stunted, rustling nightshade,
curves his palm into a cup,
points up from below,
and gives his hand a lick.

Like him,

even though my lover
neither wants nor even likes me,
just seeing him time and again
is honey to my heart.

(*Kuṟuntokai* 60, Tamil)

7.5

Is it the truth this time, Friend?
If it is, bless you.

Just as a monkey of the slopes,
face black as kohl,
errs in his leap
and crashes down with branches
too thin to bear his weight,

so my lover missed
the signal for our tryst
and my soft, round shoulders
have gone pale.

(*Kuṟuntokai* 121, Tamil)

7.6

I've long practiced knitting my brows
and batting my lashes.

With trouble, I've learned to keep from laughing,
and I've worked hard at silence.

Somehow, I've even managed to hone this mind of mine
to the point of courage.

In assuming anger,
I've girded my loins,

but success lies
in the hands of Fate.

(*Amaruśataka* 97, Sanskrit)

7.7

Tell me, Friend,
is it right,
or isn't it?

I can't bear the pain
of this hard sorrow,
and besides,
I fear the big change
called death.
Even more than that,
I wonder if that man
from the good mountain land
is afraid of the gossip
that says we're inseparable lovers.

Even at midnight
when the town huddles close and sleeps,
save for into my heart,
he doesn't even know what coming is.

(*Kuṟuntokai* 302, Tamil)

7.8

Those women
who can see their lovers
even in dreams
are lucky,

but without him
sleep won't come,
so who can dream
a dream?

(*Gāthāsaptaśatī* 4.97, Prākrit)

7.9

All I have to do
is hear his name

and every hair on my body
just bristles with desire.

When I see
the moon of his face,
this frame of mine
oozes sweat like a moonstone.

When that man
as dear to me as breath
steps close enough to me
to stroke my neck,

the thought of jealousy
is shattered in my heart
that's only sometimes
hard as diamond.

(*Amaruśataka* 59, Sanskrit)

7.10

When he has loved me,
goes but a step away
and returns
to love me again,

I'm like a wife whose husband's away,
as if for that instant
he's been exiled.

(*Gāthāsaptaśatī* 1.98, Prākrit)

7.11

Whatever patch of limb
he gazes on
with unblinking eyes,
I cover up

but I want him to see it all anyway.

(*Gāthāsaptaśatī* 1.73, Prākrit)

⁂ ⁂ ⁂

7.12

Sister,
the brackish water
at the bottom of his pond,
covered with leaves
and lapped by animals,
is sweeter than milk mixed with the honey
from our very own garden.

(*Aiṅkuṟunūṟu* 203, Tamil)

⁂ ⁂ ⁂

7.13

"Tender-limbed girl,
now this bed is all spotted
from the many piles of sandalwood dust
scattered by tight embraces."

He said this,
planted me on his chest,
first gave my lower lip
a deep bite,

then passionately
stripped off my clothes
with the scissors of his toes
and that deceiver
began to do what suited him.

(*Amaruśataka* 74, Sanskrit)

7.14

I sent that sinning man out
and when he donned my best friend's clothes
and came back,
I embraced him
by mistake;
told him a secret,
wanting to meet him.

He laughed out loud,
said, "Silly,
that would be
most difficult,"
and embraced me wildly.

That scamp
outwitted me today
at night's coming.

(*Amaruśataka* 46, Sanskrit)

7.15

The fire is quenched
by the householder's daughter,
even though the tongues of flame have spread

as she follows her man in death,
her cool limbs sweaty
from the deep joy of embracing him.

(*Gāthāsaptaśatī* 5.7, Prākrit)

7.16

As if knotted fast
at their roots,
    he somehow freed
    my arms.

As if planted
in his chest,
I, too, dug out
my breasts.

(*Gāthāsaptaśatī* 3.76, Prākrit)

7.17

Even he was abashed
and I laughed
and held him close
when he went for the knot
of my underclothes
and I'd already untied it.

(*Gāthāsaptaśatī* 4.51, Prākrit)

7.18

When my lover came to bed,
the knot came untied
all by itself.

My dress,
held up by the strings of a loosened belt,
barely stayed on my hips.

Friend,
that's as much as I know now.

When he touched my body,
I couldn't at all remember
who he was,
who I was,
or how It was.

(*Amaruśataka* 101, Sanskrit)

7.19

When my face turned toward his,
  I averted it
  and looked at my feet.

When my ears clamored
  to hear his talk,
  I stopped them.

When my cheeks broke out
  in sweat and goosebumps,
  I covered them with my hands.

But Friends,
  when the seams of my bodice
  burst in a hundred places,

what could I do?

(*Amaruśataka* 11, Sanskrit)

7.20

I don't know.

When my lover
comes to me
and says such loving things,

do all my parts
become eyes
or ears?

(*Amaruśataka* 64, Sanskrit)

7.21

Friend,
somehow
in mock anger
I told him to leave

and that hard-hearted man
left my bed,
and left with a vengeance,
just like that.

So once more,
my heart longs
shamelessly
for him.

He's ruined love
in his haste

and has cut off
all his pity.
What will I do?

(*Amaruśataka* 15, Sanskrit)

7.22

When he said,
"I'll go, I'll go,"
I mistook it
for all his former
mock departures
and I said, "Fine,
leave my side
and go away forever."

O Mother,
our master who supports us—
where is he now,
I wonder?

The place between my breasts
has filled up with tears,
has become a deep pond
where a black-legged
white heron feeds.

(*Kuṟuntokai* 325, Tamil)

7.23

Though I knit my brow,
    my gaze is fixed
    longingly
    anyway.

Though I check my tongue,
  this tortured face of mine
  dissolves
  in a smile.

Though I drive my hear to hardness,
  my body bears
  the gooseflesh
  of desire.

When I see that man,
  how on earth
  can my anger
  survive?

(*Amaruśataka* 28, Sanskrit)

⁘ ⁘ ⁘

7.24

Sighs parch my mouth.
My heart's torn out by the roots.
Sleep won't come.
I can't see my darling's face.
Day and night I cry,
and my limbs have withered
since I ignored my lover
who had fallen at my feet.

Friends,
what good were you counting on
when you made me be angry
at that dear man?

(*Amaruśataka* 92, Sanskrit)

⁘ ⁘ ⁘

7.25

I didn't long for him.
My breasts didn't heave.
The hair on my body
didn't bristle with joy.
My face didn't suddenly
bead up with sweat,

until now.

As soon as I saw
that mean, will-robbing
lord of my life,
he stole my heart.

So tell me:
by what means can this anger
which we've so cleverly planned
be set aright?

(*Amaruśataka* 84, Sanskrit)

7.26

When called,
she won't give an answer
and the bad woman is cross
with everyone for no reason
as the riverbank goes up
in smoke.

(*Gāthāsaptaśatī* 5.16, Prākrit)

7.27

Don't leer at him
with half-glances.

Look at him naturally,
so you can see him well.

That way,
you'll be taken for a virgin.

(*Gāthāsaptaśatī* 3.25, Prākrit)

∻ ∻ ∻

7.28

The slopes of your breasts
    are wiped clean of sandalpaste,
something has rubbed the color
    from your lower lip,
your mascara is a fair distance
    from your eyes
and this thin body of yours
    is covered with gooseflesh.

Liar of a go-between,
    you don't know how your friend suffers:
You left here to bathe in the pond,
    and went nowhere near that lowlife.

(*Amaruśataka* 61, Vemabhūpāla's recension, Sanskrit)

∻ ∻ ∻

7.29

"Why is your face bathed in sweat?"
    "Because of the sun's rays."
"And your red eyes?"
    "His words made me angry."

"Why are your blue-black curls such a mess?"
  "The wind did it."
"Your forehead mark? Where's that?"
  "My veil rubbed it off."
"Why are you so tired?"
  "From all my comings and goings."

"You've said it all, Messenger;
now tell me about that wound on your lower lip."

(*Amaruśataka* 93, Vemabhūpāla's recension, Sanskrit)

7.30

Aunt,

you know that Tree of Love,
its roots bound in long affection
and tended with respect?

No one heard it falling.

(*Gāthāsaptaśatī* 5.31, Prākrit)

7.31

As for me,
I am here.

My virtue lies
with boundless grief
in a salt marsh.

He is in his town

and our secret
has become gossip
in common places.

(*Kuruntokai* 97, Tamil)

7.32

If I think of him,
my heart boils

and not thinking of him
is beyond my ken.

Love hurts me—
it's so big that
it scrapes Heaven itself.

He isn't so noble,
this man I lay down with.

(*Kuruntokai* 102, Tamil)

7.33

Separation's fire
can be borne
when there's a knot of hope,
but Mother,
when my love leaves home
and stays in the same village,
it's far worse than death.

(*Gāthāsaptaśatī* 1.43, Prākrit)

Never comes back

7.34

Aunt,
how can I tell him,
with my heart about to burst?

Like an image on a mirror,
my pain will not enter him.

(*Gāthāsaptaśatī* 3.4, Prākrit)

❖ ❖ ❖

7.35

That man
who kissed me with zeal
when my face was smeared
with *ghī* and pigment

has no energy to touch me now
even though I'm all decked out
with jewels.

(*Gāthāsaptaśatī* 6.19, Prākrit)

❖ ❖ ❖

7.36

When the bond of love broke,
the respect born of affection withered,
good feelings fled,
and that man walked before me
like any other,

Good Friend,
I imagine all this
think on days gone by

and wonder why
my heart hasn't cracked
into a hundred bits.

(*Amaruśataka* 43, Sanskrit)

7.37

People who tell me
to bear my love,

don't they know about love,
or are they that strong?

Since I can't see my lover,
my heart swells
with hidden sorrow
and like a flood in spate
fading to a streak of foam
as it dashes against stones,

slowly,
slowly I turn to nothing.

(*Kur̲untokai* 290, Tamil)

7.38

. . . And that wanderer will come home,
and I will get angry,
and he will win me back.

All this
only when it comes to some other girl's lover.
The garland of *her* heart's wishes
blossoms and bears fruit.

(*Gāthāsaptaśatī* 1.17, Prākrit)

7.39

I gave up shame,
lost my virginity
and became notorious
for his sake.

Dear Friend,
this same man
has now become
some other person.

(*Gāthāsaptaśatī* 6.24, Prākrit)

⁂ ⁂ ⁂

7.40

"This is black, darling."
  "Yes, it's black."
"No, it's white."
  "Ah, so it is."
"We'll go."
  "We're going."
"I don't want to go."
  "Then so be it."

That's the way it was before.
For the longest time,
he'd wander down any path
my mind wished to take,
but now this same man
has become another.

Friend,
is there anyone
who knows a thing about men?

(*Amaruśataka* 94, Sanskrit)

8

The Advice of Older Women to Their Young Friends

"Love's Ways Are Like This, as Curled as the Tendrils of New Cucumber"

·:·:· The nineteen poems in this chapter depict responses made by girlfriends to the requests, complaints, and concerns expressed by the young women in the preceding section. The narrative in this section unfolds with an older confidante's address to a guileless heroine, marking the moment at which the older, more experienced woman notices the stirrings of love manifested by her younger friend's gestures and glances. Poems 8.2–8.7 are composed on a theme that was quite popular with the poets of all three traditions, that of an older confidante dispensing words of wisdom and encouragement to her young friend. Poem 8.4, a Prākrit *gāthā,* is a sample "script" provided by the confidante to the heroine in order to instruct her; readers will see enactments of this ploy in later sections, ripened into mature arguments between unhappy men and women. In poems 8.8–8.12, the confidante chides the heroine when she has taken her anger and pouting a bit too far. The *Amaruśataka* verses in this group—numbered 8.8, 8.10, and 8.11—are particularly fine examples of this theme. Poems 8.13–8.15 serve as exquisite examples of a popular context in which a confidante advises a particular type of heroine found in Sanskrit and Prākrit convention, the *abhisārikā,* a woman who is preparing herself for a secret meeting with her lover under the cover of darkness. The stunning simile in poem 8.14, a Prākrit *gāthā*, serves to praise the heroine's fair complexion as well as to encourage the young woman in her romantic endeavors. In poems 8.16–8.19, the older confidante again dispenses sage advice. The Prākrit *gāthās* in this group, numbered 8.16, 8.17, and 8.19, are observations that the confidante makes to a group of her own peers, to a young pregnant wife, and to a new bride, respectively. Poem 8.18, a longer Tamil narrative poem from *Naṟṟiṇai*, records the words of a confidante to a heroine in the *pālai* landscape of abject separation.

8.1

Looking sideways,
melting over and over with love,
opening and shutting
like buds,

for an instant,
your eyes glance at him
and quivering with shame,
look away
as if signaling
some stirring of love
deep down in your heart.

Tell us,
Young Girl,
who is that lucky man
you're looking at now?

(*Amaruśataka* 4, Sanskrit)

❖ ❖ ❖

8.2

You long only for his chest.

May you live long, Friend.
Don't be brokenhearted:

Like the ancient Kōcar warriors
who took an oath,
cut down King Naṉṉaṉ's
fragrant mango tree
and overran his land,

all we need now
is a little hard-hearted scheming.

(*Kuruntokai* 73, Tamil)

❖ ❖ ❖

8.3

Women who play an innocent game
will snatch your lover away
and won't stop it even if prevented.

So why do you waste away   *Stop moaning.*
and cry uselessly?   *Go get him back.*
Don't do these girls any favors.

He's handsome
and has a taste for love.
He's young, he's sophisticated—
your man is like that,
Timid Girl.

So why don't you
win him over
with pretty sarcasms?
That way,
you can buy him back.

(*Amaruśataka* 8, Sanskrit)

❖ ❖ ❖

8.4   → "*Script*"

Calm down, darling.
    Who's angry?
You are, slim girl.
    So what's anger to a stranger?

So who's a stranger?
    You are, Master.
And how is that?
    Due to the powers of my wicked deeds.

(*Gāthāsaptaśatī* 4.84, Prākrit)

8.5

Why are you crying
with your head bent down
as the rice fields turn white?

The hemp field's like a dancer,
face daubed with yellow paint.

(*Gāthāsaptaśatī* 1.9, Prākrit)

8.6

Why are you confused
over old deeds we have done?

Live long, Friend,
and don't sorrow.

We'll go.
We'll tell him,
and come back.
So get up
and look here.

Like that nectar from the sea
with its rows of waves,
the salt that faces rain,

I fear that you'll dissolve
and melt away.

Facing their man's cruelty to us,
their love for us is great
and they just can't bear it.
Friend,
those fruit-shedding hills of his
will weep waterfalls
of tears.

(*Nar̲r̲iṇai* 88, Tamil)

❖ ❖ ❖

8.7

Friend,
don't cry
with the moon of your face
turned away.

Love's ways are like this:
as curled as the tendrils
of new cucumber.

(*Gāthāsaptaśatī* 1.10, Prākrit)

❖ ❖ ❖

8.8

Surely in these parts,
there are young girls
in house after house.
Now go and ask them
if their lovers bow down before them
like your slave does.

You're torturing yourself.

Let the endless prattle
of backbiters
go in one ear
and out the other.

Men become cut off
from their taste for love,
and are only brought round again
with effort.

(*Amaruśataka* 91, Sanskrit)

❖ ❖ ❖

8.9

Friend,

with ums and ahs,
vacant attention,
and shakes of your head
you punctuate our every word
when you're not busy sighing.

Why are you bothering us?

(*Gāthāsaptaśatī* 4.56, Prākrit)

❖ ❖ ❖

8.10

Your husband's outside,
downcast,
scratching on the ground.

Your friends won't eat—
their eyes are swollen
from all their crying.

The pet parrots have quit
all their silly recitations,
and just look at the shape you're in.

Hard-hearted Girl,
get rid of this jealousy
now.

(*Amaruśataka* 7, Sanskrit)

8.11

You haven't weighed the consequences
for your love,
nor have you any regard
for your friends.
Why are you making
such a fuss now, Prude,
when it's too late?

With your own hands
you've brought down upon yourself
these coals,
their blazing points of flame
as bright as Doomsday Fire.

So enough now
of your crying
in the wilderness.

(*Amaruśataka* 80, Sanskrit)

8.12

He fell at your feet,
    and you ignored him.
He said loving things,

and you spoke without love.
Even when he left,
you didn't stop him.

So tell me:
for whose sake
is all this fuss?

(*Gāthāsaptaśatī* 5.32, Prākrit)

8.13

You've strung your breasts
with a rattling rope of pearls,
tied a jangling belt
around those deadly hips
and clinking jeweled anklets
on both your feet.

So, Stupid,
if you run off to your lover like this,
banging all these drums,
then why
do you shudder with all this fear
and look up, down,
in every direction?

(*Amaruśataka* 31, Sanskrit)

8.14

You'll soon be by his side, Lovely,
don't hurry.
Let the moon rise.

Who can see your face in the moonlight,
like milk in milk?

(*Gāthāsaptaśatī* 7.7, Prākrit)

⁂ ⁂ ⁂

8.15

"Girl with thighs
as curved as the flat of my palm,
where are you off to
in this dense dark of night?"

"To the place
where my darling man lives,
dearer to me
than my own life."

"But child,
you're alone.
Tell me why
you aren't afraid."

"No doubt
the God of Love,
armed with feathered arrows,
will escort me."

(*Amaruśataka* 71, Sanskrit)

⁂ ⁂ ⁂

8.16

The red of her lower lip
kissed off by her lover at night
can be seen at dawn,
reflected in the eyes
of other wives.

(*Gāthāsaptaśatī* 2.6, Prākrit)

8.17

A daughter-in-law's heart
is not as choked by the heavy weight
of the child in her womb

as it is by not being allowed
to straddle her man
in sex.

(*Gāthāsaptaśatī* 5.83, Prākrit)

8.18

Even though he takes my hands
and presses them to his eyes;
takes up his own hands,
strokes my good forehead
and speaks sweet words like a mother,
he's a thief,
a cruel man,

that lord of the mountains
where the hills have tall peaks
and on the summits
the tall, swaying stems
of bamboo with green nodes
cleave passing clouds
on the ranging mountain slopes
spread with golden kino flowers
where waterfalls drop
like a stream of sapphires.

(*Naṟṟiṇai* 28, Tamil)

8.19

They take abuse
  with smiles,
their hardship
  with great ceremony,
their quarrels
  with tears:

This is the path of good women.

(*Gāthāsaptaśatī* 6.13, Prākrit)

⁂ ⁂ ⁂

9

Friends Carry Messages to the Lovers

"Now Aren't You Afraid of the Spear in Her Father's Hand?"

The twenty poems in this chapter build on the various contexts depicted in chapters 7 and 8—the lovers have asked their friends to act as go-betweens to carry messages for them. The poems grouped here represent a tangled constellation of communication: 9.1–9.16 depict a variety of situations in which the confidantes of young, unmarried women carry messages to their lovers (or would-be lovers). This section opens with a highly unusual poem from the Tamil anthology *Naṟṟiṇai,* in which the confidante tries to discourage a persistent man from courting a girl who is from a lower social class. The anonymous author has drawn richly from elements found commonly in the *neytal* landscape, that of the seashore, the context of emotional discord and lament. Poems 9.2–9.6, all Prākrit *gāthās,* are superb examples of a witty confidante who artfully praises her young friend's extraordinary beauty in the man's presence (9.2 and 9.3), then tries to arrange a meeting between the lovers (9.4–9.6; see my exegesis of poem 9.5 in chapter 1).

Poems 9.7–9.11 depict the popular theme of the confidante's attempt to patch things up between the quarreling lovers, reporting to the man the heroine's wretched condition, either real or feigned. Poems 9.12–9.15 continue in this vein. The man is about to leave on an extended trip, and the confidante pleads with him on her friend's behalf, quoting the heroine's words to him directly in poem 9.14. In poem 9.16, from the Tamil anthology *Aiṅkuṟunūṟu,* the confidante urges the hero to hurry up and marry her friend.

Poems 9.17–9.19 are the words of the *hero's* female confidante carrying messages to his intended. In his headnote to poem 9.18, a Prākrit *gāthā,* commentator Gaṅgādharabhaṭṭa writes: "In order to instill kindliness in a woman who was dissatisfied because she hadn't been given ornaments and the like, a go-between spoke of her regard for absolute love by means of indirect description." Like poem 9.18, poem 9.19 is also a clever little lesson in the impermanence of wealth. Gaṅgādharabhaṭṭa writes, "The idea is, 'Since mundane existence is impermanent like this, then why do you shun the pleasure of union with a lover who is as skilled as this one?'" The final poem in this section serves as a frank reminder to the hero from a male friend, pointing out to him that if a silly omen is enough to stop him from undertaking a journey, then why not his beloved's own tears?

9.1

This girl
lives in a small
pleasant village
near the shore,
a daughter of fishermen
who pierce and stir up the water
of the big blue sea
as they kill fish.

And you?
You're from that old market town
where long banners shiver
in the breeze,
a beloved son
of a rich man
with fast chariots.

What is your beauty to us,
who want the dried meat
we slice from fat sharks
as we sit and scare off
flocks of birds?

We reek of fish,
so get ready to leave.

The good little lives
that we make for ourselves
from the fruits of the sea
are not like yours
and among us, too,
there are fine men to be had.

(*Naṟṟiṇai* 45, Tamil)

9.2

Even in a reeling world
as great as this,
teeming with thousands
of gorgeous women,

nothing at all compares
to her right half
save for her left.

(*Gāthāsaptaśatī* 4.3, Prākrit)

9.3

How can you describe her?

When your gaze falls
on one of her parts,

like a sick cow fallen
in mud,

it cannot escape.

(*Gāthāsaptaśatī* 3.71, Prākrit)

9.4

She scatters
the lotuses of her eyes
up the street,
waiting for you to come,

resting her breasts on the gate
like a pair of auspicious pots.

(*Gāthāsaptaśatī* 2.40, Prākrit)

9.5

Her husband,
given to jealousy,
won't let her gather
honey flowers
at night,

but Mother,
that simpleton
will go and do it
all by himself.

(*Gāthāsaptaśatī* 2.59, Prākrit)

9.6

Son of the village chief,
you're pitiless,
scared of your wife
and as difficult to see
as a worm in a neem fruit.

The village is starving itself over you
in spite of it all.

(*Gāthāsaptaśatī* 1.30, Prākrit)

9.7

You gave your love to her
  all by yourself.
You've petted this girl for an eternity
  all by yourself,
and now,
due to a twist of fate,

you've committed some new crime
  all by yourself.

She can't bear her jealousy
and it's clear
that sweet talk
just isn't going to work.
So, Scoundrel,
let's let our friend
cry out all her sorrow.

(*Amaruśataka* 6, Sanskrit)

9.8

Lucky Man,
she can't find room
in your heart
filled with a thousand women.

She has nothing better
to do with her days,
so she makes her thin body
even thinner.

(*Gāthāsaptaśatī* 2.82, Prākrit)

9.9

It's all your fault, Boy.

That wretch sits endlessly
on the threshold
and in just one day

has withered
like a garland of welcome.

(*Gāthāsaptaśatī* 3.62, Prākrit)

9.10

She willed her endless tears to her kin,
delivered her anxiety to her parents,
left her misery entirely to her servants,
and pledged her fever to her girlfriends.

Her sighs have depleted her
and on this day or next,
she will enjoy the highest of freedoms.

So be calm:
She has parceled out all
her separation-born sorrow.

(*Amaruśataka* 78, Vemabhūpāla's recension, Sanskrit)

9.11

Calmed by my pleading,
she continued to list your crimes,
found that her fingers weren't enough
and cried forever.

(*Gāthāsaptaśatī* 3.77, Prākrit)

9.12

Even by noon
of the very first day,
she'd etched the wall
with lines, counting

he left today,
he left today,
he left today.

(*Gāthāsaptaśatī* 3.8, Prākrit)

9.13

Because of neglect, Son,
though well-forged
in affectionate bonds,
Love in time
will trickle away
like water through cupped hands.

(*Gāthāsaptaśatī* 3.36, Prākrit)

9.14

Listen, Friend,
and live long:

Because a fine-winged heron
balanced on a swaying mastwood branch
spurns the tiny fish
in the wide salt marsh
and craves the blue lilies
fragrant with nectar
in the fields with their spears of rice,

when you see that cool and handsome man,
don't chide him.
Don't dare to ask him
if it's right for him
to leave that girl with the bangles
when she's in a state like this.

(*Kuṟuntokai* 296, Tamil)

9.15

A tear
black with mascara
looks like a measuring string
on her heart,
about to be cleft in half
by the saw
of unbearable separation.

(*Gāthāsaptaśatī* 2.53, Prākrit)

9.16

O Man from the fields
where the waterbird calls out
to his keening mate,
I say to you:

You come all the time to our big house
while the whole place is asleep.
Now aren't you afraid of the spear
in her father's hand?

(*Aiṅkuṟunūṟu* 60, Tamil)

9.17

Lovely,
this plowman's son
with the good-looking wife
has gone so thin over you
that the woman,
though jealous,
is playing the go-between herself!

(*Gāthāsaptaśatī* 1.84, Prākrit)

9.18

They live everywhere
on forest grass and water
that they've taken for themselves

and even then,
the love of a buck and his doe
ends only in death.

(*Gāthāsaptaśatī* 3.87, Prākrit)

9.19

There were those young men,
those village lands
and that youthfulness of mine.

People now tell it
like a tale
that I must listen to.

(*Gāthāsaptaśatī* 6.17, Prākrit)

9.20

A solitary black-spotted deer
walking on your right
will stop you from leaving home,

but what about your love's two eyes,
all muddy with tears?

(*Gāthāsaptaśatī* 1.25, Prākrit)

10

Young Men Speak to Their Male Friends

"Suddenly She Showed Me Favor with a Tear"

This small cluster of eleven poems shows men conversing with their peers in various modes and for various reasons. This chapter opens with an exquisite and moving example from the Tamil anthology *Kuruntokai,* set in the *kuriñci* context, that of love in union. The man has fallen in love with a young girl, and they have met and have made love in secret in the forest. According to U. Vē. Cāminātaiyar, the man's companion has ridiculed his lovesick friend, and he speaks this lovely poem in response (see chapter 1 for a fuller exegesis).

All of them Prākrit *gāthās,* poems 10.2–10.9 depict a worldly man who wittily shows off his knowledge of sex and women for his companion as they travel down the road together. Compare the remembered kiss of poem 10.4 (the woman is menstruating) with poem 7.35; here we get the male perspective. The last two poems are fine examples of descriptions of reconciliation from the Sanskrit *Amaruśataka.*

10.1

I wonder
if I'll ever touch her again.

Her elder brothers have fine bows
and they whistle and toss stones
to flush an innocent, sad-eyed doe
from her cover and separate her
from her herd in the wide-spaced forest.

She stands before them
as they plunge red-shafted arrows
into the breast
of her raging, swift buck
and rip them out with blood.

That girl from the hills,
her hair dark and fragrant,
has black-rimmed eyes
shaped like those arrowheads,
points placed opposite each other

and I wonder
if I'll ever again touch
those shoulders of hers.

(*Kuṟuntokai* 272, Tamil)

❖ ❖ ❖

10.2

"Tonight,
I must go to that lucky man
and in the blinding dark."

Thinking that,
a respectable woman,

eyes squeezed shut,
practices walking in her house.

(*Gāthāsaptaśatī* 3.49, Prākrit)

10.3

Her face is like the moon.
Her mouth tastes like the drink of life.
Her wild, hot kiss
with a pull of her hair
is like . . .
what?

(*Gāthāsaptaśatī* 3.13, Prākrit)

10.4

Her face was smeared
with *ghī* and turmeric
and I remember that kiss:

lip carefully thrust out,
brows, noses not touching.

(*Gāthāsaptaśatī* 1.22, Prākrit)

10.5

When the plowman fled,
having left a highborn woman for dead
in her throes of pleasure,

the cotton plant
bobbed with the weight

of new bloom on its stalk
as if laughing.

(*Gāthāsaptaśatī* 4.60, Prākrit)

10.6

Her man falling asleep,
limp from dragging a plow sunk in mud,
the slattern curses the rains,
her pleasures unfinished.

(*Gāthāsaptaśatī* 4.24, Prākrit)

10.7

The straw that she mockingly gave
to the traveler for bedding

was dragged away at dawn
as that highborn woman wept.

(*Gāthāsaptaśatī* 4.79, Prākrit)

10.8

The bad wife sobs
and heaps up the last
of the honey-flower blossoms—
so hard to look at,
as if they're the bones
of a friend
from a pyre.

(*Gāthāsaptaśatī* 2.4, Prākrit)

10.9

Seeing the naive bride's breasts
which had begun to swell
in a big way,

the first wife,
her cheeks withered,
heaves a sigh.

(*Gāthāsaptaśatī* 4.82, Prākrit)

10.10

"He's been lying here at your feet
for a good long time.
Fool, aren't you just being contrary?

"What damage has he done?
What blame is on this man who loves you?
He's just a little slow."

As the edge to her anger softened
when her friends told her this,
afterwards, she suddenly burst into tears
and couldn't stay, but neither could she go.

(*Amaruśataka* 68, Sanskrit)

10.11

When jealousy faded
and the moon of her face
was borne by her hand,

when there was no way out
for me other than to
drop at her feet,

suddenly
she showed me favor
with a tear,
    caught in a space
    between the fringes
    of her lashes,

a tear
    that broke, scattered
    on the slope
    of her breast.

(*Amaruśataka* 25, Sanskrit)

11

Young Men Speak to Their Lovers

"Anger Has Become Your Lover, Not I"

·:·:· This group of seven poems opens with four fine verses from the Sanskrit *Amaruśataka* in which the man begs his beloved for forgiveness (it is unclear in some of these verses whether the pair are married or unmarried lovers). This particular theme is a favorite among Sanskrit poets, and it is one greatly favored by the poets anthologized in the Amaru collection especially. Compare poem 11.2 with poem 11.4, a Prākrit *gāthā,* keeping in mind their contexts and the suggestion that we can understand such verses to be "studied arguments." Poem 11.5 is a lovely example of Prākrit pillow talk, and 11.6 an artful piece of flattery, addressed simultaneously to the man's beloved and the moon. This poem is a simple but beautiful sample of innovation within the bounds of sometimes rather tired convention, this verse being an inversion of the common simile, "Your face is like the moon." This section ends with a Tamil poem from *Kuṟuntokai,* in which the man offers tender premarital reassurance to his lover.

11.1

You've erased the tracery
on your cheek
by covering it with your palm.

Your sighs have kissed away
the juice of your lower lip,
tasty as nectar

and at every instant,
the tear that's stuck in your throat
is making your sloping breasts tremble.

  Unkind Girl,
  Anger has become your lover,
  not I.

(*Amaruśataka* 81, Sanskrit)

11.2

My girl.
  Yes, lord?
Get rid of your anger, proud one.
  What have I done out of anger?
This is tiresome to me.
  You haven't offended me.
  All offenses are mine.
So why are you crying yourself hoarse?
  In front of whom am I crying?
In front of me.
  So what am I to you?
You're my darling.
  No, I'm not.
  That's why I'm crying.

(*Amaruśataka* 57, Sanskrit)

11.3

Hard-hearted girl,
get rid of these doubts
based on false rumor.

It's not good
to subject me to sorrow
because of backbiters' words,

or have you decided now,
silly girl,
that it's all true?

Do to me what you will,
sweetheart.

Suit yourself.

(*Amaruśataka* 53, Sanskrit)

11.4

You got up to meet me,
all smiles,
even from a distance.

I placed my orders
on your head,
and you gave respectful answers

but in union,
your look never softened,
and my heart's on fire.

Hard-hearted Girl,
your anger's tucked away inside
and this is all a sham.

(*Amaruśataka* 14, Sanskrit)

11.5

Your hair is as messed as a peacock's tail,
thighs are trembling,
eyes half-closed.

You've been playing the man a little
and you want to rest.

So consider the trials of men!

(*Gāthāsaptaśatī* 1.52, Prākrit)

11.6

The full moon
cannot gain
a likeness to your face,
so god destroys it
time and again,
as if to create it
by some other means.

(*Gāthāsaptaśatī* 3.7, Prākrit)

11.7

My mother and your mother,
what are they to each other?

My father and your father,
  what proper kinsmen are they?

And you and I—
  how did we come to know each other?

Like red earth and streaming rain,
our loving hearts merged
all by themselves.

(*Kuṟuntokai* 40, Tamil)

12

Women Speak to Their Lovers

"Who Can Show Somebody the Workings of the Heart by Tearing It in Two?"

The eighteen poems in this chapter are all from the Prākrit anthology *Gāthāsaptaśatī:* they all are direct addresses from women to their lovers. The Prākrit language (especially the Prākrit of this anthology, Māhārāṣṭrī) was regularly used by poets and dramatists to represent the manner in which women and children speak—it is softer and spoken in indistinct murmuring tones—but is also chosen to express the thoughts and artifices of women embroiled in illicit affairs because it is a language that promotes ambiguity and multiple interpretations. It is used as a vehicle to represent feminine wit and indirection of speech. This section opens with two poems in which the heroine directly expresses her jealousy and envy to her lover. Poems 12.3–12.7 record women's words as they quarrel and complain to their men; the commentators place poem 12.4 in the mouth of a married woman who is expressing her disgust for her own husband to her lover.Poems 12.8 and 12.9 are spoken by clever heroines as they drop hints to potential lovers. Poem 12.10 is quite unusual (compare it to poem 7.15). Commentator Gaṅgādharabhaṭṭa writes that these are the words of a woman who is "commenting on the passionate nature of women in general, in order to steal away her lover's heart." Poems 12.11 and 12.12 serve as indirect indications to the man that favorite trysting spots have been wrecked; the latter poem is the address of an unfaithful wife to her lover. Poem 12.13 is spoken by a sexually experienced heroine to her clumsy lover, and poem 12.14 is obviously an early Prākrit model for some of the poems on a similar theme found in later Sanskrit collections. Please see chapter 5 for interpretations for poems 12.15–12.18, which, according to Gaṅgādharabhaṭṭa, are spoken by the woman to her lover *in flagrante delicto* to help him "last longer."

12.1

If that slut
stepped on your foot
just to get out of the muck,
then, Lucky Man,
why all this gooseflesh now?

(*Gāthāsaptaśatī* 1.67, Prākrit)

❖ ❖ ❖

12.2

Lucky Man,
 it's true that she's virtuous
 and has a beautiful body.

And it's true that I'm lacking.

But tell me:
 will all these people
 who aren't like her
 have to die?

(*Gāthāsaptaśatī* 6.11, Prākrit)

❖ ❖ ❖

12.3

Love goes
 when he's not around,
 goes
 when he's around too much,
 goes
 because of idle rumor;
 goes
 all by itself.

(*Gāthāsaptaśatī* 1.81, Prākrit)

12.4

Even the hatred
in a man
who's valued for his learning
is desirable,

but I'm shamed
by even love
in a person
who's reviled by others.

(*Gāthāsaptaśatī* 3.67, Prākrit)

12.5

In separation,
a lover's burgeoning grief
just can't be ended
without the pleasures of death.

(*Gāthāsaptaśatī* 4.49, Prākrit)

12.6

Lucky Man,
be sure of this.

Your crimes
don't burn me
as much as these clever words
empty of all good feeling.

(*Gāthāsaptaśatī* 4.53, Prākrit)

12.7

You show up
and you rattle off endearments.

Lucky Man,
that's where your goodness stops,
and tell me this:

Who can show somebody
the workings of the heart
by tearing it in two?

(*Gāthāsaptaśatī* 5.89, Prākrit)

❖ ❖ ❖

12.8

At whom can I make eyes?

To whom can I tell
  my pleasures and pains?

With whom can I joke
  in this wreck of a village
  overrun with fools?

(*Gāthāsaptaśatī* 2.64, Prākrit)

❖ ❖ ❖

12.9

The wretched night
is dark as pitch.

Today my husband's gone away
and the house is empty.

So, Neighbor,
stay awake.

That way,
no one will steal me.

(*Gāthāsaptaśatī* 4.35, Prākrit)

12.10

Her limbs washed in sweat
from the pleasuring touch of ash
left from her lover's cremation,

a novice ascetic cannot finish
smearing her body with it.

(*Gāthāsaptaśatī* 5.8, Prākrit)

12.11

Dear Friend,

the canebrakes
nestled in the riverbank's lap
their clusters broken
from the weight of blue bees,
have in time
become stumps.

(*Gāthāsaptaśatī* 5.22, Prākrit)

12.12

The mean dog is dead,
my mother-in-law is crazy
and my husband's gone away.

Who's to tell him
that a buffalo
has wrecked the cotton, too?

(*Gāthāsaptaśatī* 6.49, Prākrit)

12.13

Even elegant
and practiced sex
from shrewd men
won't sweep me off my feet

as will love made
in goodness and affection
wherever or however done.

(*Gāthāsaptaśatī* 3.74, Prākrit)

12.14

You've squeezed your eyes shut
in false sleep
and your limbs bristle with desire
when I kiss your cheek.

O Lucky Man,
make room for me in bed—
I won't waste time anymore.

(*Gāthāsaptaśatī* 1.20, Prākrit)

12.15

With the cooing of pigeons
nesting on roof pegs
that you can barely see,

the temple moans in pain
as if pierced by a spike.

(*Gāthāsaptaśatī* 1.64, Prākrit)

12.16

Look,
  a still, quiet crane
  shines on a lotus leaf
  like a conch shell lying
  on a flawless emerald plate.

(*Gāthāsaptaśatī* 1.4, Prākrit)

12.17

Look,
  a spider clings
  by its upturned legs
  to its own silk,
  hanging from the thatch
  like a lone bakula blossom
  strung on gossamer thread.

(*Gāthāsaptaśatī* 1.63, Prākrit)

12.18

Look,
  rubies and emeralds mixed
  fall from heaven
  like a necklace unstrung
  from the throat of the sky goddess:

A line of parrots.

(*Gāthāsaptaśatī* 1.75, Prākrit)

13

The Lovers Muse to Themselves

"Grow Long, Blessed Night"

The twenty poems included in this chapter represent the words of women and men in solitude, speaking to themselves, to their own hearts, to the moon; sighing out their desires, regrets, and memories into the blank, lonely night. The first seven poems are spoken by women and are quite straightforward in expression and meaning. The remaining poems are all spoken by men (the commentators occasionally remark that these poems are either "spoken by the hero to his own heart, or alternatively, to a male confidante" or to a travelling companion. Poems 13.8 and 13.9 are the words of men who are totally undone by the artifices and charms of their lovers. Poems 13.10 and 13-11, the first a Prākrit *gāthā*, the second a Tamil poem from *Kuṟuntokai*, reflect the heroes' befuddlement at finding their lovers bold by night, but shy or indifferent by day. Poems 13.12–13.18 are all heroes' recollections—either tortured or fond, sometimes both—of past sexual pleasures, of returning to their homes to embraces after long journeys, and of acutely painful moments of parting. Poem 13.19 is a man's soliloquy about his lover's growing indifference, and the final poem, from the Tamil anthology *Kuṟuntokai*, is an outburst of despair set in the *marutam* landscape, that of horrible quarreling and infidelity after marriage. According to U. Vē. Cāminātaiyar, the speaker has been consorting with other women, and he speaks this poem to his own heart but within earshot of his wife.

13.1

My bangles left.

My best friends, tears,
went on forever.

My self-control
wouldn't sit still for a minute.

My mind made itself up
to go on ahead.

When my man
made up his mind to go,
everything else went,
just like him.

Life,
if you must go, too,
then don't forsake
your entourage of friends.

(*Amaruśataka* 35, Sanskrit)

13.2

If you're going to burn, burn.
If you're going to boil, boil
and if you're breaking, Heart,
go ahead and break,

for I've just left him,
that no-good man.

(*Gāthāsaptaśatī* 5.1, Prākrit)

13.3

I am that same willing girl
and these two anklets
are the same two
that went to men for sex.

I am the one who's poor now
among us womenfolk,
our natural-born modesty
being our wealth.

So, when I straddled him,
ashamed when my memory came back,
I panicked
and recognized my own slender body.

First I gave up on my masculine ways.
Then I gave up on him.

(*Amaruśataka* 89, Sanskrit)

13.4

Fool that I was,
  why didn't I caress
  that precious man's neck?

When he kissed me,
  why did I lower my face?

Why didn't I look at him?

Why didn't I talk to him?

  Thinking back on her gestures
  as a new wife,

a young girl regrets it,
having since savored the delights
of love on the rise.

(*Amaruśataka* 58, Sanskrit)

13.5

Groveling,
intimate words,
heart-stealing flattery,
a tight embrace
of my thinner-than-thin body,
violent kisses all over—

obviously,
getting angry is worth the risk,
but even still,
I'm not interested.

My lover
is dear to my heart,
so how could I be like that
on purpose?

(*Amaruśataka* 95, Sanskrit)

13.6

The anger
that my friends
planted in my heart
when they somehow found
a hole in it

ran off
  like an illicit lover
  as soon as I saw my man.

(*Gāthāsaptaśatī* 2.44, Prākrit)

13.7

They say that my donkey-hearted lover
might leave home tomorrow.

Grow long, Blessed Night,
so that for him
tomorrow just won't be.

(*Gāthāsaptaśatī* 1.46, Prākrit)

13.8

Expecting me to grovel,
  she carefully covers both feet
  with the hem of her skirt.

She pretends to hide
  a coming smile
  and won't look straight at me.

When I talk to her,
  she chats with her friend
  in cross tones.

Even this slim girl's rising anger
  delights me,
  let alone her deep love.

(*Amaruśataka* 47, Sanskrit)

13.9

She's just a kid,
  but I'm the one who's fainthearted.
She's the woman,
  but I'm the coward.
She bears that high, swollen set of breasts,
  but I'm the one who's burdened.
The heavy hips are hers,
  but I'm unable to move.

It's a wonder
how clumsy I've become
because of flaws
that shelter themselves
in another.

(*Amaruśataka* 34, Sanskrit)

13.10

When we made love,
she issued hundreds of orders
and her cheeks bloomed with joy,
but at dawn,
this same woman hangs her head
and I'm not so sure she's my lover.

(*Gāthāsaptaśatī* 1.23, Prākrit)

13.11

My lover
is a thief
who knows two things:

In the dense dark of night
she comes smelling
of the forests of Muḷḷār
that belong to red-speared Malaiyan̲
who is strong in battle,

and she's on my side,

but at daybreak,
she shakes out those mixed flowers
she had worn in her hair,
daubs oil on her head
that had smelled of fired sandal
and wears an indifferent face.

Then, she sides with her kin.

(*Kur̲untokai* 312, Tamil)

13.12

Her breasts
  were dwarfed
  in a tight embrace.
The hair of her body
  bristled with desire.
That cloth
  on her glorious hips
  melted away
  in the heat
  of the moment
and with weak words
she urged me,
  "Don't, don't,
  thief of my pride,
  don't. For me,
  it's more than enough."

Then I don't know—
was she asleep,
or dead?
Did she merge
with my heart?
Did she dissolve
into nothing?

(*Amaruśataka* 40, Sanskrit)

13.13

Her face faded, pale,
starved,
pinched from starvation,
tired,
curls all slack

found its luster again
the instant
I'd returned
from abroad
unexpected.

I just can't describe
that slim girl's proud mouth,
its wonderful taste
at the time we made love
and what I reverently drank from it.

(*Amaruśataka* 88, Sanskrit)

13.14

If I weigh the world
hugged by vast seas

of spreading waves
and god's land
of hard-to-get splendor,

the two together
are not equal in value
to the moment when
I held that girl,

her black-rimmed eyes like flowers,
her skin like gold,
her private parts
with their good folds,
our opposite shoulders
touching.

(*Kuṟuntokai* 101, Tamil)

13.15

"Don't travelers meet up again, Lovely?"
Don't worry on my account.
You've gone completely thin."

When I said this to her,
my eyes full of tears,
she looked at me,
her pupils dulled with shame.

She choked back her tears
as they fell,
and with a laugh,
showed her zeal for instant death.

(*Amaruśataka* 10, Sanskrit)

13.16

From the mango tree
at the border of the courtyard garden,
she's plucked a blossom
adorned with humming female bees
addicted to its dense and flowing pollen.

I imagine that
the young girl
has veiled her thin body
with a piece of her upper cloth,
her rising sighs
make her breasts shake
and, trembling,
she stifles the sound
in her throat.
She's crying.

(*Amaruśataka* 78, Sanskrit)

13.17

Her sad eyes staring at my path,
my darling's tears
must be sizzling
as they fall
on the slopes of her creamy breasts,
her heart burning
with rows of flame
from the fire of a long separation.

(*Amaruśataka* 86, Sanskrit)

13.18

She's in the house.
She's at turn after turn.

She's behind me.
She's in front of me.
She's in my bed.
She's on path after path,
and I'm weak from want of her.

O heart,
there is no reality for me
other than she she
she she she she
in the whole of the reeling world.

And philosophers talk about Oneness.
(*Amaruśataka* 102, Sanskrit)

13.19

She's cross, but doesn't pick fights like she used to
  when I untie her clothes,
nor does she furrow her brow or gnaw at her lip
  when I grab her by her hair.
She gives me her limbs on her own,
  and doesn't twist out of my rough embrace.

  But this slender girl has learned
  some other type of anger.
(*Amaruśataka* 63, Vemabhūpāla's recension, Sanskrit)

13.20

Like the poor flowerless head
of a penniless lute player
without his patron Evvi,

Heart, may you live long
and grieve on in sadness.

That woman,
her thick dark hair smelling
of the night-blooming jasmine
on the tree near our house—

who is she to me?

(*Kuṟuntokai* 19, Tamil)

14

The Voices of Mothers and Foster Mothers

"Her Hair Not Even Long Enough to Tie in a Knot"

⁖ The following eleven poems are all spoken by mothers and foster mothers who are pining for their young daughters after they have eloped with their lovers. All of these poems are from the Tamil anthologies—the convention of mothers' lamentations is utterly unique to Tamil poetics. The poets of this tradition had a finely tuned sense of how parents fit in with the erotic lives of their children. The first two poems are spoken by the young girl's foster mother *(cevili-t-tāy)*. In poem 14.1, the foster mother sets out in search of the eloping couple and gives voice to her despair, and in poem 14.2, the foster mother comforts the bereft and grieving biological mother *(naṟṟāy)* and says prayers for the eloping couple's comfort as they make their way across the desert wastelands appropriate to the *pālai* landscape, that of abject and sometimes permanent separation. Poems 14.3–14.8 are culled from a decad of verses found in *Aiṅkuṟunūṟu, makaṭ-pōkkiya vaḻi-t-tāy iraṅku pattu,* "the decad of the mother's lamentations at the elopement of her daughter." She complains about the gossip her daughter's rash actions have caused, curses the young man's mother for ever having given birth to him, describes the utter foolishness of her daughter, who has gone traipsing off to forests so tangled that even the monkeys stay out of them, and remarks bitterly on the name that her daughter's friends have given her.

Poem 14.9 is spoken by the mother to the foster mother about the never-never land of elopement, central to the understanding of the conventions of *pālai*, a landscape only to be traversed and never dwelt in. Poems 14.10 and 14.11, parallel verses from *Kuṟuntokai* and *Naṟṟiṇai* respectively, allow the grieving mother to express her own wonder at the stamina of her own daughter.

14.1

My feet have stumbled;
my eyes have looked and looked
and lost their light.

There are more couples
in this world
than there are stars
in the black and widening sky.

(*Kuṟuntokai* 44, Tamil)

⁂ ⁂ ⁂

14.2

Leaving us behind,
our dark, simple girl crosses the desert
with that young man, his spear long and flashing.

Let cool rains fall today,
on the sands overspreading
their narrow path through the mountains
under the shade of trees
impenetrable by the rays of the sun.

(*Kuṟuntokai* 378, Tamil)

⁂ ⁂ ⁂

14.3

Accompanied by the youth
who persuaded her heart
with promises,
my girl has crossed over
many lush hills,

causing gossip to rise
in this noisy old town.

Has she given me so much as a thought?

(*Aiṅkuṟunūṟu* 372, Tamil)

14.4

May she be in agony whenever she thinks of it,
the mother of that youth,
his strong bow of bamboo,
who led my daughter
through the heat of the desert
where a buck with branching antlers,
fleeing a tiger's spring,
bellows out to his doe.

(*Aiṅkuṟunūṟu* 373, Tamil)

14.5

If I ponder it many times,
these two things make sense:

That girl,
her hair not even long enough
to tie in a knot
and protected by that youth of godlike strength,

is that very same girl
who crossed the wilds of the forest
that the monkeys don't even know.

(*Aiṅkuṟunūṟu* 374, Tamil)

14.6

I will not grieve for that girl
who left us along with our tears
in the evenings
when a bat in its struggle to go
unfurls its wings
and soars.

But I will grieve for her friend,
her lovely eyes rimmed in black,
her heart now full of pain
without her sweet-tongued companion.

(*Aiñkuṟunūṟu* 378, Tamil)

14.7

Uniting with the man
with the gleaming white spear,

is going through the forests
where herds of bull elephants roam
on dew-covered slopes
sweeter to her
than the pleasure
of a good marriage
in the company of her dearest friends,
I wonder?

(*Aiñkuṟunūṟu* 379, Tamil)

14.8

With strength's help,
I have taken the name

"The mother of that stupid girl
with the budding smiles
and teeth white as pearls
who ran off with her lover
down long jungle trails."

Her very own friends
call me that!

(*Aiṅkuṟunūṟu* 380, Tamil)

14.9

How your love for your daughter stings you!

Our beloved, pretty girl
has crossed the forest
in a place that spans two countries,
saddening us,
making our empty hearts grieve to the point
that our lives are so starved that they leave us,
right along with all our lush sorrow and pain.

(*Aiṅkuṟunūṟu* 313, Tamil)

14.10

A man who wears a hero's anklet
keeps her safe as she hurries
through scant, dry lands
where the shade shrinks and dies.
At the bank of a scorched pool,
she sips at muddy, steaming water.

Where does she find the strength,
this girl, soft as a sprout,
with her tiny, curving bracelets?

She had refused even to touch milk
mixed with fine, puffed rice
in a bowl clad in blushing gold
that I'd held out for her,
saying that it was too much.

(*Kuṟuntokai* 356, Tamil)

14.11

I held in one hand
a pot of glowing gold
full of sweet milk,
white and tasty,
mixed with honey.
I ordered her to eat,
and as I beat her,
raising a small rod
with a soft tip
wound round with cloth,
she toddled away,
her golden anklets clattering
with their fresh-water pearls inside.

That little prankster,
who ran under a canopy
so that the good, old foster mothers,
their hair gray and thinning,
would slow down and stop in their tracks,
where did she learn this knowledge,
these manners?

As her husband's family grows poor,
she doesn't think once
of the rich rice her father used to give

and more adaptable
than running water
in fine black sand,
she eats when she can,
that little one
with such great strength.

(*Naṟṟiṇai* 110, Tamil)

15

Wives Address Their Philandering Husbands

"More Than There Are Bees Sucking Honey from Budding Flowers"

The fifteen poems in this chapter all represent the voices of unhappy wives (the commentaries attached to a few of these verses suggest that the speakers could also be unmarried women who are lashing out at inconstant lovers). This section opens with two poems that depict protesting wives as their husbands set out on long journeys. Poem 15.1, a Prākrit *gāthā,* is a bit opaque in meaning, but commentator Mathurānāth Sāstrī offers this interpretation, adopting the voice of the wife: "Whoever might be cut off from my heart for just an instant would naturally be remembered. But a man who lives night and day in my heart, how can I remember him?" The point seems to be that a love that lives in memory is not a love worth having! Poem 15.2, from the Sanskrit *Amaruśataka,* ends in a bald suicide threat. Poem 15.3, a Tamil verse from *Kuṟuntokai,* is addressed to a crowing rooster (but meant for the husband's ears). Since this unusual poem is set in the *marutam* landscape, we can surmise that the husband has been sleeping with other women but has decided to return home. Poems 15.4–15.10 all record the voices of women as they bitterly quarrel with their men. All of these poems (with the exception of poem 15.4, a Prākrit *gāthā*), are from the Amaru collection and demonstrate the pure genius of the authors associated with this anthology—their ability to create monologues and dialogues such as these, employing highly complex, algebraic meters while maintaining a perfectly colloquial tone, is unparalleled in other South Asian literary traditions. The final six poems all directly allude to rivals. Verses 15.10 and 15.11, from the Tamil anthology *Aiṅkuṟunūṟu,* are spoken by a woman whose body has been ruined by childbirth. Her husband has taken on lovers, and she shames him. This is a theme that is unique to the Tamil tradition. The final poem in this series, a Prākrit *gāthā,* is spoken by a senior wife. She says this obliquely to her husband, who has focused all of his affections on a new co-wife. The senior wife compares herself to a serviceable, durable shawl that is warm in winter—what good is an ox against the cold?

15.1

Of course
I can remember a man
who strays from my heart
for all of an instant,

but when it's a love I have to remember,
what's the use?

(*Gāthāsaptaśatī* 1.95, Prākrit)

❖ ❖ ❖

15.2

With tears rolling,
oath taking,
prostrations,
and endearments,

those other wretches forbid
the lords of their breaths
to travel,

but I'm virtuous.
Go.
Good luck,
and good day to you,
as you set out at dawn.

You'll hear about
whatever steps I take
that fit our love, dear,
after you've left.

(*Amaruśataka* 61, Sanskrit)

❖ ❖ ❖

15.3

Rooster,
ruler of the flock,
    your thick red crest
    like the lustrous blooms
    of Malabar lilies
    with their dense clusters,

may you suffer torture
and become bits for the larder
of a young wildcat
who hunts down house rats
in the dense dark of midnight.

You're the one
who woke me from
my sweet and guarded sleep
as I lay with the man
from the town
that gleans wealth
from wide waters.

(*Kuṟuntokai* 107, Tamil)

15.4

I'm on my half of the bed,
my face turned away,
and my heart's aflame with regret.

So why do you burn my back, too,
with your hot sighs?

(*Gāthāsaptaśatī* 1.33, Prākrit)

15.5

At first, my breasts, barely swelling on my chest,
    fully ripened as they met yours.

My prattle completely lost its simplicity
as if mixed with your filigreed words.
The vines of my arms let go my nurse's neck
and clung fast to your own.

Rude man, now that my street
is one you no longer wander down,
what am I to do?
(*Amaruśataka* 87, Vemabhūpāla's recension, Sanskrit)

15.6

Stop these promises, dear.
I've had enough
of your pointless chatter.
Go away.
It's not your fault
in the least,
it's Fate who's turned
his back on me.
If your love
has ripened
and fallen
to this state,
then what's pain to me
when my useless life
leaves me,
flimsy as it is?
(*Amaruśataka* 30, Sanskrit)

15.7

Because you wander in
every single morning
at sunrise,

wakefulness
is born
in both my eyes.

I'm weak.

Whatever weight I've borne with you
has vanished
and I've grown thin.

You've done all you can
and I've given up
my fear of death,

so go.
It's hard for you
to stand here
and whatever cure
I take now
you'll hear about
later.

(*Amaruśataka* 33, Sanskrit)

15.8

When anger
was a crease in the brow
and silence
a catastrophe,

when making up
was a mutual smile
and a glance
a gift,

now just look at this mess
that you've made of that love.

You grovel at my feet
and I berate you
and can't let my anger go.

(*Amaruśataka* 38, Sanskrit)

15.9

At first,
our bodies were as one.

Then
you were unloving,
but I still played the wretched favorite.

Now
you're the master
and we're the wife.

What's next?

This is the fruit I reap
from my diamond-hard life.

(*Amaruśataka* 69, Sanskrit)

15.10

O Man from the place of new wealth
with its great watertank,
where a crane perches atop
a myrobalan in the field
and gorges himself on paddy fish,
your women are pure and fragrant.

We are like a demon.
We gave birth to a child.

(*Aiñkuṟunūṟu* 70, Tamil)

15.11

I'm not angry, so tell me without lying:

She who snatched away
your return in your chariot
to your fertile house,
even when you'd thought of your son
with his unsteady steps—

who is that woman, Lord?

(*Aiṅkuṟunūṟu* 66, Tamil)

15.12

Cheat, even while embracing me,
you heard the rattle of her jeweled belt
and instantly slackened the knot of your arms.

My friend, reeling from the poison
of your many words made of honeyed butter,
doesn't even notice me.

To whom can I tell my troubles?

(*Amaruśataka* 73, Sanskrit)

15.13

O Man of the place
where an otter, stinking of flesh,
catches a scabbard fish for his daily meal
in a place near the tank,

even if it wrecks our beauty,
we will not cling to a chest, Lord,
that has been embraced by others.

(*Aiṅkuṟunūṟu* 63, Tamil)

15.14

Listen:
That woman you've taken now is gullible.

They say that she's proud
of her own great beauty
which rivals mine,
but I cannot rival her.

Many have dulled her hair
and her bright forehead,
more than there are bees
sucking honey from budding flowers.

(*Aiṅkuṟunūṟu* 67, Tamil)

15.15

A low man
will trade his shawl
for an ox
in the dead of winter,
looking at the breasts
of that dusky girl
as if they're smokeless embers.

(*Gāthāsaptaśatī* 3.38, Prākrit)

16

Wives Speak to Their Husbands' Messengers and to Their Friends

"Going Like an Arrow Spat by a Bow"

The seventeen poems in this series are set in two slightly different contexts. The first four poems are addressed to the husbands' (or lovers') messengers. Poems 16.1 and 16.2, from the Tamil anthology *Aiṅkuṟunūṟu,* are from a decad devoted to reeds. Set in the *marutam* landscape, reeds represent rival women. The reed stalks chafe and tear at delicate mango threads and lotus petals, which symbolize the wife as well as happy, fertile domesticity in general. The speaker of poem 16.4, a Prākrit *gāthā,* betrays her passion to an elderly woman. Commentator Mathurānāth Śāstrī's headnote reads, "Having seen the extreme depression of her nephew, an aunt took it upon herself to act as a go-between, and as she listed the man's qualities, his beauty, and so on, the heroine, her passion for him aroused, said this to her."

Poems 16.5–16.17 are all addressed to the confidantes of wives. Poem 16.5, a Prākrit *gāthā,* on first glance seems to be a straightforward profession of love, but Mathurānāth Śāstrī provides the following interpretation for this verse in a headnote: "A certain chaste wife whose husband was abroad spoke thus of her deep love for him, sending back a wicked go-between who was desirous of bringing her own wishes to fruition." In poems 16.6–16.8, jilted wives seek comfort in their friends, and angry but proud and witty women are the speakers in verses 16.9–16.11. Poem 16.10, a Prākrit *gāthā*, is an answer to a comment passed by a confidante. According to commentator Gaṅgādharabhaṭṭa, the confidante states, "Beautiful women win men over with emotion, even though it's false." The witty wife then speaks the *gāthā* in response. The remaining poems are all spoken by abandoned wives who are longing for their men.

16.1

That man is from the place
where white reed-flowers in cool groves
tear at the pale threads
of the mango tree growing in a dune,
its thick branches reeking
of the scent of lovers' bodies.

Because of this, my eyes smart,
shedding tears like blossoms in the rain.

(*Aiñkuṟunūṟu* 19, Tamil)

16.2

Thinking of that man
from the place near the riverbank
where tubular reeds, like bamboo hollows,
rip out eggs laid in a hundred-petaled lotus
by a fine-winged bee with its six tiny legs,

the beautiful, gleaming bangles
slip from my wrists.

(*Aiñkuṟunūṟu* 20, Tamil)

16.3

Even if he lived in the same town,
he wouldn't come to our place.

Even if he came here
he wouldn't hug me fully.

He'd walk right past
without looking

as if I were some burning ground
for strangers.

Wrecking my modesty,
Love has shed its good sense
and is lost in the distance,
going like an arrow spat by a bow.

(*Kuṟuntokai* 231, Tamil)

16.4

Aunt,
I drank him in
for all of a second,
and I wasn't satisfied

as if my thirst could be quenched
by water drunk
in a dream.

(*Gāthāsaptaśatī* 1.93, Prākrit)

16.5

His form is fixed in my eyes,
his touch in my limbs,
his whispers in my ear,
and his heart is kept in my heart.

So what can Fate tear in two?

(*Gāthāsaptaśatī* 2.32, Prākrit)

16.6

That man from the place
where a speckled crab scrabbling in mud
burrows under a root
of a thorn bush—
he spoke sweet words, married me;
said he'd never leave.

What has happened now, Mother?

(*Aiṅkuṟunūṟu* 22, Tamil)

⁂ ⁂ ⁂

16.7

Aunt,
there's no such thing
as honest love
in the world of men.

If there were,
who'd separate?

And if separation ever came to be,
who could go on living?

(*Gāthāsaptaśatī* 2.24, Prākrit)

⁂ ⁂ ⁂

16.8

Even if my chastity is dead,
my beauty blighted,
and my sweet life ebbs away,

don't tell him, Friend.

He's like Mother and Father to us now,
isn't he?

Why sulk
when there is no love?

(*Kuṟuntokai* 93, Tamil)

⁂ ⁂ ⁂

16.9

Listen, Friend, and live long:

Because that man came to our house
for all of a day,
they say that his women wailed for seven,
their hearts softening instantly
like wax in fire.

(*Aiṅkuṟunūṟu* 32, Tamil)

⁂ ⁂ ⁂

16.10

A man who knows the Real
is won only by true feeling.

Who can fool an old cat
with sour gruel?

(*Gāthāsaptaśatī* 3.86, Prākrit)

⁂ ⁂ ⁂

16.11

At first she rubs it,
then washes it
and then

the stupid young thing
slaps at the nailprint
her lover left
on her breast.

(*Gāthāsaptaśatī* 5.33, Prākrit)

16.12

That man from the lush riverbank
where the reed with its row of flowers
chafes the fertile shoots
of the nearby mango tree with its soft fruit—

his chest makes a cool bed full of sweet grace.

(*Aiṅkuṟunūṟu* 14, Tamil)

16.13

Now without him,
I remember all the pleasures tasted.

The rumble of new clouds
sounds like an executioner's drum.

(*Gāthāsaptaśatī* 1.29, Prākrit)

16.14

I don't see any mango buds,
Mother-in-Law,
and the wind
with that Malabar smell
isn't blowing,

but my longing alone says
that spring has come.

(*Gāthāsaptaśatī* 6.42, Prākrit)

16.15

He got up and said,
"I'm going,"
and I fearlessly listened.

As he went off into the distance,
I ignored him,
even though he turned back
time and again
and stood stock-still in the road.

Again,
I will stay in this house
that's bereft of him.
These breaths of mine
are holding fast.
Friends, stay with me.
I'm fond of living.
These tears
are just for show.

(*Amaruśataka* 79, Sanskrit)

16.16

Friend,
tell us.

We ask you
with good feeling:

Why do the bangles
on the wrists
of every woman
grow larger
when their lovers
leave home?

(*Gāthāsaptaśatī* 5.53, Prākrit)

❖ ❖ ❖

16.17

When the sun goes,
    the heavens flush red,
    grief sharpens,
    the light dies
    and jasmine blooms,

only the confused will say it's evening.

For even when the crested cock crows
in the town's long hallways
and the great darkness fades,

dawn is evening.

Broad daylight's evening
to those who have no one.

(*Kuṟuntokai* 234, Tamil)

17

Wives' Friends Speak to Husbands' Messengers (and to the Husbands Themselves)

"Just Where Does Your Chariot Think It's Going?"

The first four poems of this chapter are spoken by the confidantes of abandoned wives to their husbands' messengers. In every case, these words are said and then carried to the husbands to impel them to hurry home. Poems 17.5–17.19 are all addressed directly to the husband. Verses 17.5–17.7 are oblique instructions to husbands who are clumsy or overeager, or who don't quite understand the importance of conjugal happiness. The tropes of the man-as-bee/woman-as-jasmine-bud are popular, almost overexploited metaphors in Prākrit and Sanskrit convention. In poem 17.8, the confidante tells the husband how much his newly pregnant wife loves him. Poems 17.9–17.13 are all from the Tamil tradition. The confidante quotes the wife verbatim to the husband, and it is unclear whether this is a time-honored convention or a latter-day commentarial "intervention"—it is possible that U. Vē. Cāminātaiyar and other modern Tamil commentators were uncomfortable with the idea of such direct confrontations between quarreling husbands and wives.

Poems 17.14–17.17 can only be interpreted as scolds. Poem 17.14, from the Tamil anthology *Aiṅkuṟunūṟu,* contains an oblique and fascinating hint to the husband. Through the dogged repetition of the word "red," the confidante is indicating to the inconstant man that his wife is menstruating and that he should turn his chariot around and return to his wife as soon as possible to make full use of her ensuing fertile period. The final two poems are the confidante's exasperated pleas to the husband to make up with his wife.

17.1

Her husband gone,
the daughter-in-law
made even her wrathful
mother-in-law weep
when she bowed at her feet
and both bangles
slipped down.

(*Gāthāsaptaśatī* 5.93, Prākrit)

❖ ❖ ❖

17.2

Like a life-giving drug for her son,
the mother-in-law,
with nothing else to do,
watches over his wife
whose life had leapt to her throat
when she saw new clouds.

(*Gāthāsaptaśatī* 4.36, Prākrit)

❖ ❖ ❖

17.3

Look, Poet,
at something
that has real beauty:

when new, white moonlight
spread through the evening
a hero sighed
the sigh of a sleepy elephant
and lay in a nest of flowers
on a short-legged cot.

He embraced his son with love
and his son's mother
embraced his back.

(*Kuṟuntokai* 359, Tamil)

17.4

She shut her eyes
and imagined her lover on the bed,

hugged herself tight
with her own loose-bangled arms.

(*Gāthāsaptaśatī* 2.33, Prākrit)

17.5

The weight of its body
cleverly suspended
by its own wings,

the bee
sips at the bud
of the night-blooming jasmine,

opening it,
greedy for its juice.

(*Gāthāsaptaśatī* 5.42, Prākrit)

17.6

O bee,
yoked with greed
for a drink of sap,

the jasmine bud
hasn't even opened
its petals
in the least,
and yet
you rub against it.

(*Gāthāsaptaśatī* 5.44, Prākrit)

17.7

The bride's mother
was pleased at the sight
of a tooth mark seen
on a thigh revealed
when her daughter's skirts
were lifted by the wind,

as if she'd seen the mouth
of a jar full of treasure.

(*Gāthāsaptaśatī* 6.7, Prākrit)

17.8

Her girlfriends asked that innocent,
"What? What appeals to you?"
when her first pregnancy cravings appeared.

Her gaze merely fell
on her husband.

(*Gāthāsaptaśatī* 1.15, Prākrit)

17.9

That man from the shores
with their spreading waters

where a big flock
of small white red-mouthed crows
stays in a grove thick with flowers,
hating the cold
when a spray
cast up by waves
soaks their wet backs to the skin:

If he leaves me,
my friend,
other than my own sweet life,
is there any other thing
that we will lose?

(*Kuṟuntokai* 334, Tamil)

17.10

Even though farmers
will clear a field
and leave blue lilies to wither
on long ridges
so their fragrance
meant for the bees
will leach into the ground,
the flowers don't think,
"Cruel men.
Let's change fields
and grow elsewhere."

Great Man,
I'm like the lilies of your town
that will bloom again

in a forbidding field.

Though you've done me many wrongs,
I don't have the strength
to live without you.

(*Kuṟuntokai* 309, Tamil)

❖ ❖ ❖

17.11

Your place is ornamented by a river
that gives cool, cloudy water in autumn;
if it's summer, it takes on
the clear sheen of sapphires—

but my eyes, Lord,
are only adorned with yellow film.

(*Aiṅkuṟunūṟu* 45, Tamil)

❖ ❖ ❖

17.12

At one time
if my friend gave you
a hard, green neem fruit,
you would have called it
a sweet, soft lump of sugar.

But now,
even if she gives you
clear water from that bracing pool
on Pāri's Paṟampu Hill
and gives it cold in winter,
you'd say that
it was hot and brackish.

Sir, this is your kind of love.

(*Kuṟuntokai* 196, Tamil)

17.13

If you play in water long enough,
your eyes will redden
and in the mouth of a glutton,
even honey will sour.

If you don't love me,
then lead me
to my father's house
with its fine, cool pond
where you snatched me
from the misery
of my trembling fear
when poisonous snakes
writhed in the road.

(*Kuṟuntokai* 354, Tamil)

17.14

As a young red-lipped woman grieves,
the whites of her cool eyes streaked red,
her red fingers stained a deeper red
from stringing garlands
of red purslane tendrils,

just where, O Chieftain,
does your chariot think it's going?

(*Aiṅkuṟunūṟu* 52, Tamil)

17.15

Love is sinister,
  is mean to us in separation;
  makes our thin bodies thinner.

This fellow Death
  lacks mercy
  and is good at counting our days.

And Master,
  you, too, are subject
  to the plague of jealousy

so think:
  how could womenfolk,
  soft as sprouts,
  live like this?

(*Amaruśataka* 67, Sanskrit)

❖ ❖ ❖

17.16

"The days have outnumbered
my fingers and toes.
What can I count with now?"

Saying this,
the naive girl cries.

(*Gāthāsaptaśatī* 4.7, Prākrit)

❖ ❖ ❖

17.17

I saw this, Sir,
and now that I've seen you,
what can I do?

I saw those women
with their fine jewels
who had taken a place on your chest,
waiting to see you

on the lovely road
where a fine, small lute
in the hand of a bard
drones with the hum of a young bee;

I saw their teardrops,
falling hot as their sorrows ripened;

I saw them
as they pulled and pulled
at your chest,
as if it were a plank
that many grab
as they panic and tumble
with a boat that capsizes
in the sea at a bad time
when the wind is strong;

I saw them
in their state of lasting, growing misery.

Yes, I saw all this, Sir,
and now that I've seen you,
what can I do?

(*Naṟṟiṇai* 30, Tamil)

17.18

Listen, Lord, and live long:

I served as medicine
to end your sorrow;
to soothe your confused heart.

But now, I am no medicine for this girl,
and my heart is suffering.

(*Aiṅkuṟunūṟu* 59, Tamil)

⁂ ⁂ ⁂

17.19

Life is only transient.
Youth, once gone, doesn't return.
Days are not the same as other days.

So why are people cruel?

(*Gāthāsaptaśatī* 3.47, Prākrit)

18

The Voices of Other Women

"Like Water Boiled, Then Cooled, Love's Taste Goes Flat"

This book ends with a group of eight poems, all of them spoken by the "other women" in the love triangles that have been so well described in many of the previous chapters. The designation "other woman" includes all kinds of women, actually: lovers, concubines, courtesans, prostitutes, and elderly madams. The first three poems in this series, all of them from the Prākrit *Gāthāsaptaśati,* are spoken by old bawds. In poem 18.1, an elderly whore teases a young lover about his habitual trips to the riverbank for trysts. Poem 18.4, from the Tamil anthology *Aiṅkuṟunūṟu,* is spoken by a *parattai,* literally "another woman," to her confidante "within earshot of the wife's companions," according to U. Vē. Cāminātaiyar's gloss. In poem 18.5, a love-weary courtesan speaks in eloquent despair to her procuress, and in poem 18.6, a Prākrit *gāthā,* the other woman, using the ruse of addressing a honey flower bush, suggests an ideal meeting place to her lover. According to the commentators, poem 18.7 is an address made by an "unchaste" woman to her own heart. Poem 18.8, however, is the most achingly poignant of the lot—a bitter, lonely boast made by the other woman to her lover's companions as his wife gives birth to a boy.

18.1

Boy,
you've made a habit
of cutting flowers.

The gods will be satisfied
with handfuls of water.

So don't go to
the Godāvarī's banks.

They'll uproot your virtue.

(*Gāthāsaptaśatī* 4.55, Prākrit)

18.2

I'm telling the truth.

I'm standing at death's door
and even today
my sight falls
on that thicket
on the Tāptī's pure banks,

just as before.

(*Gāthāsaptaśatī* 3.39, Prākrit)

18.3

Those friends have left.

Only stumps remain
in the thickets

and we've grown old, besides.

Love's been cut off
at the roots.

(*Gāthāsaptaśatī* 3.32, Prākrit)

18.4

Listen, Friend, and live long:

He is expert in lying
to the women who want him,
as their painted eyes dim
and fill with tears,

but he doesn't know a thing
about making a sworn oath real.

(*Aiṅkuṟunūṟu* 37, Tamil)

18.5

When love is broken
then patched up
and cruelty is obvious,

like water boiled,
then cooled,
its taste goes flat.

(*Gāthāsaptaśatī* 1.53, Prākrit)

18.6

Honey Flower
in your tangled thicket

on Godāvarī's banks,
your branches touching the ground,
bent low with your load of blossoms,
listen to my plea:

You'd better shed your flowers slowly.
(*Gāthāsaptaśatī* 2.3, Prākrit)

18.7

Heart,

you're running at will,
roaming down paths in the sky
after someone who is playing hard-to-get.

One of these days,
you'll burst.
(*Gāthāsaptaśatī* 3.2, Prākrit)

18.8

As a bright, long-clappered bell
echoed in the guarded house
and women with fine ornaments
stood as good omens to one side,
like great bards keeping watch over a hero
under the canopy where sand was spread
and thatched leaves rustled,

as the son slept, smelling of birth,
with his nurse on a soft couch
spread with scented cloth
and as the lovely wife closed her moist lids,

her body soft, her beauty damp
from a bath in fresh oil blended
with seeds of white mustard,

that man from the town
with its wide waters
came home like a thief
in the thick black of night

and that's the way he was born,
that boy who bears the name
of his noble grandfather.

(*Naṟṟiṇai* 40, Tamil)

Notes

Chapter 1: Introduction

1. See Daniel H.H. Ingalls's introduction to *An Anthology of Sanskrit Court Poetry: Vidyākara's "Subhāṣitaratnakoṣa,"* Harvard Oriental Series, vol. 44 (Cambridge: Harvard Oriental Series, 1965), pp. 44–45.

2. For the rather intricate problems of dating Tamil texts, see Kamil Zvelebil, *The Smile of Murugan on Tamil Literature of South India* (Leiden: Brill, 1973), pp. 23–41.

3. Siegfried Lienhard, *A History of Classical Poetry: Sanskrit/Pali/Prakrit* (Wiesbaden: Otto Harrassowitz, 1984), p. 81.

4. All translations are my own unless otherwise indicated.

5. Zvelebil, *Smile,* p. 62.

6. Earl Miner, "Some Theoretical and Methodological Topics for Comparative Literature," *Poetics Today* 8, no. 1 (1987): 138.

7. Paul Dundas, "The *Sattasaī* and its Commentators," in *Indologica Taurinensia* (Torino: Instituto di Indologia, 1985), 17:8.

8. See V. Raghavan, ed., *Śṛṅgāramañjarī of Saint Akbar Shah* (Hyderabad: Hyderabad Archaeological Department, Hyderabad Government, 1951), p. 54.

9. See Bhaṭṭa Mathurānāth Śāstrī's introduction to his edition of the *Gāthāsaptaśatī* (1933; reprint, New Delhi: Motilal Banarsidass, 1983), pp. 16–18.

10. *Sragdharā* is one of the more complex classical Sanskrit meters, containing twenty-one syllables per line.

11. A separate school of criticism does not exist for Prākrit poetry. All critical material that I use in my discussions of Prākrit poetry comes from critics who wrote in Sanskrit and employed Sanskrit critical terms and methodology.

12. Zvelebil, *Smile,* p. 52.

13. N. Subrahmanian, *Pre-Pallavan Tamil Index* (Madras: University of Madras, 1966), p. 6.

14. "Four Hundred Poems on *Puṟam* Themes." *Puṟam,* "outer," is complementary in meaning to *akam* and in this context refers to poems that are about public life, especially politics and warfare.

15. Zvelebil, *Smile,* pp. 131–149.

16. K. Paramasivam, personal communication, Madurai, July 15, 1990. For his arguments, please see his article titled "Relative Chronology of *Tolkāppiyam* and Early Sangam," in *Studies in Dravidian Linguistics,* ed. S. Vaidyanathan and Jardiljeet Singh Sidhu, Pakha Sanjam, vol. 10 (Patiala: Panjabi University, 1980). *Studies in Dravidian Linguistics,* no. 1.

17. Takanobu Takahashi, *Tamil Love Poetry and Poetics* (Leiden: Brill, 1995), pp. 20–24.

18. Lienhard, *Classical Poetry,* p. 93.

19. Dundas, *"Sattasaī,"* p. 9.

20. Miner, *"Theoretical and Methodological Topics,"* p. 129.

21. The final chapter of the *Tolkāppiyam,* which is on the usage of words and the categorization of things according to how many senses they have.

22. Zvelebil's translation, *Smile,* p. 247. This seems to indicate that Old Tamil was not just a language reserved for literary composition or for the erudite of certain classes, as was Sanskrit.

23. Ibid., p. 252.

24. This poem was composed by Pōtaṉar in *pālai-t-tiṇai,* the "landscape of the desert tract," which denotes separation in its most extreme form. See *Kuṟuntokai* 44, 356, and 378 and also *Aiṅkuṟunūṟu* 313, as well as the decad titled *makaṭ-pōkkiya vaḻi-t-tāy iraṅku pattu* ("the decad of the mother's lamentations at the elopement of her daughter") for other examples of this particular *pālai* genre.

25. See R. Periakaruppan, *Tradition and Talent in Cankam Poetry* (Madurai: Madurai Publishing House, 1976), p. 279.

26. The Sanskrit line reads: *śiśulīlānartanacchadmatālapracala-valayamālāsphālakolāhalena.*

27. This appears to be the most widely accepted date. P. V. Kane places the composition of this text between 100 B.C.E. and 300 C.E. See his *History of Sanskrit Poetics,* 4th ed. (New Delhi: Motilal Banarsidass, 1971), p. 424.

28. As formulated in the sixth chapter of the *Nāṭyaśāstra.* The whole process is much more complicated than this. Please see chapters 2 and 4 for somewhat more technical explanations.

29. K. Paramasivam, personal communication, Madurai, August

1990. The author of this section of the *Tolkāppiyam* never makes this clear.

30. See *Tolkāppiyam: Poruḷatikāram Piṟpakuti,* with the commentary of Pērāciriyar, ed. K. Cuntaramūrtti (Annamalainagar: Annamalai University, 1985), p. 10. I am grateful to the late K. Paramasivam for providing me with guidance through this difficult passage.

31. K. Paramasivam, personal communication, Madurai, November 1990.

32. The author is Oruciṟai-p Periyaṉ. The landscape is identified as *kuṟiñci,* that of love in union, because the initial sexual encounter between the speaker and his lover has already taken place. This is an example of a popular *kuṟiñci* theme in which the speaker begins to think of ways to secure a second meeting with the beloved.

Chapter 2: Reading "North" and "South"

1. Jonathan Culler, "Literary Competence," in *Reader-Response Criticism: From Formalism to Structuralism,* ed. Jane P. Tompkins (Baltimore: Johns Hopkins University Press, 1980), p. 102.

2. See Daniel H.H. Ingalls's introduction to *The "Dhvanyāloka" of Ānandavardhana with the "Locana" of Abhinavagupta,* trans. Daniel Ingalls, Jeffrey Masson, and M. V. Patwardhan (Cambridge: Harvard University Press, 1990), p. 19.

3. Ibid., p. 18.

4. As listed in *Nāṭyaśāstra* 6.15. Some lists include a much debated ninth *rasa*, that of tranquillity *(śānta)*.

5. *Vibhāvānubhāvavyabhicārisaṃyogād rasaniṣpaiḥ*.

6. Ingalls, introduction, p. 18.

7. Ibid., pp. 16–17.

8. As listed in *Nāṭyaśāstra* 7.93.

9. Commentarial headnotes will be provided throughout the book in this same fashion whenever they are available and/or relevant to the discussion.

10. They are love on sight, attachment of the mind, brooding, insomnia, emaciation, aversion to objects, shamelessness, insanity, swooning, and death.

11. Ingalls, introduction, pp. 36–37.

12. Norman Cutler, *Songs of Experience: The Poetics of Tamil Devotion* (Bloomington: Indiana University Press, 1987), p. 61.

13. Ibid.

14. The eighth chapter of the *Poruḷatikāram*, "the Chapter on the Subjects of Composition," an early semiotics of poetry.

15. *uyttuṇarvu iṉṟi-t-talaivaru poruḷāṉ/meyppaṭa muṭippatu meyppāṭu ākum.*

16. Takanobu Takashi, *Tamil Love Poetry and Poetics* (Leiden: Brill, 1995) pp. 20–24. Kamil Zvelebil, *The Smile of Murugan on Tamil Literature of South India* (Leiden: Brill, 1973), pp. 138–149.

17. Cutler, *Songs*, p. 61.

18. S. Ilakkuvanar, *Tholkāppiyam in English with Critical Studies* (Madurai: Kural Neri Publishing House, 1963), p. 244.

19. The italics are mine.

20. P. S. Subrahmanya Sastri, *Tolkāppiyam: The Earliest Extant Tamil Grammar: Text in Tamil and Roman Scripts with a Critical Commentary in English*, pts. 1–3, "*Poruḷatikāram:* Tamil Poetics" (Madras: Kuppuswami Sastri Research Institute, 1959), p. 67.

21. *Akattiṇaiyiyal* verse 13 states: "The things that are not behavioral elements may overlap," meaning that everything except for the behavioral elements may.

22. A. Nārāyaṇacāmi Aiyar, commentator, *Naṟṟiṇai Nāṉūṟu* (1952; reprint, Ceṉṉai: Tirunelvēli Teṉṉintiya Caivacittānta Nūṟpatippu-k-Kaḻakam, 1976), p. 152.

23. It has been suggested to me that the difficult phrase *ciṟu-veṇ kākkai-c-cev-vāy-p-perun-tōṭu*, "big flock of small white red-mouthed crows," may be referring to albinism and that the crows have been ostracized by the far more common black members of their own species. Further, references to "white crows" occur in the Sanskrit epic and are usually employed metaphorically to indicate that some thing or situation is unusual, inverted, or wrong. But this particular image of the white crow is probably drawn from common human observation. During a downpour, crows often ruffle their feathers, revealing a silvery down, and this is much more in keeping with the Tamil poetic system, which is, after all, based on practical and naturalistic description rather than on abstract symbolism.

24. A. K. Ramanujan, *Poems of Love and War from the Eight Anthologies and the Ten Long Poems of Classical Tamil* (New York: Columbia University Press/UNESCO, 1985), p. 238.

25. See George C.O. Haas's introduction to *The "Daśarūpa": A Treatise on Hindu Dramaturgy by Dhanaṃjaya* (New York: AMS Press, 1965), p. xxi.

26. Ibid., p. 131.

27. Ingalls, introduction, p. 264.

28. Georges Poulet, "Criticism and the Experience of Interiority," in *Reader-Response Criticism: From Formalism to Structuralism*, ed. Jane P. Tompkins (Baltimore: Johns Hopkins University Press, 1980), p. 43.

29. Ibid.

30. See Jacques Lacan, "The Mirror Stage as Formative of the Function of the I as Revealed in Psychoanalytic Experience," in *Écrits: A Selection*, trans. Alan Sheridan (New York: Norton, 1977), pp. 1–7.

31. Ingalls, introduction, p. 11.

32. K. Kunjunni Raja, *Indian Theories of Meaning* (Madras: Adyar Library and Research Centre, 1963), pp. 277–278.

33. Paul Dundas, "The *Sattasaī* and Its Commentators," in *Indologica Taurinensia* (Torino: Instituto di Indologia, 1985), 17:9.

34. Jonathan Culler, "Literary Competence," in *Reader-Response Criticism*, p. 111.

35. Terry Eagleton, *Literary Theory: An Introduction* (Minneapolis: University of Minnesota Press, 1983), p. 174.

36. Culler, "Literary Competence," p. 110.

Chapter 3: Reading Tamil *Caṅkam* Poetry

1. Kamil Zvelebil, *The Smile of Murugan on Tamil Literature of South India* (Leiden: Brill, 1993), p. 248.

2. K. V. Jagannathan, *U. V. Swaminatha Iyer* (New Delhi: Sahitya Akademi, 1987), p. 38.

3. N. Subrahmanian, *Pre-Pallavan Tamil Index* (Madras: University of Madras, 1966), p. 6.

4. See the previous section for a translation and discussion of the first few verses of the *Akattiṇaiyiyal*. These verses set forth the dimensional (space/time) and environmental aspects of Tamil *akam* poetry.

5. Naṉṉaṉ is the name of any of a number of minor chieftains. See Subrahmanian, *Tamil Index*, pp. 484–485.

6. This poem was composed by Paraṇar. The *tiṇai* is identified as *kuṟiñci*, "love in union."

7. This is one of the most common *kuṟiñci* situations. One general requirement of a *kuṟiñci* poem is that sexual intercourse must have taken place at least once.

8. Subrahmanian, *Tamil Index*, p. 334.

9. It is likely that Paṟampu Hill, described in *Puṟanāṉūṟu* 109 as a naturally bountiful place, was a site of one of Pāri's victories. The word *paṟampu* means "beating" or "thrashing."

10. *Puṟanāṉūṟu* 112 is attributed to these very daughters.

11. This poem is by Naṉṉākaiyār, composed in the *tiṇai* called *neytal,* that of the seashore. The usual context in *neytal* is of a woman lamenting her lover's absence.

12. A famous chieftain of Takaṭūr.

13. This poem is Auvaiyār's work. Auvaiyār, whose name simply means "Granny," is *cañkam*'s most accomplished and prolific woman poet, and perhaps the most accomplished of *all* the *cañkam* poets, male or female. She composed many poems in both *akam* and *puṟam*.

14. Zvelebil, *Smile,* p. 103.

15. Terry Eagleton, *Literary Theory: An Introduction* (Minneapolis: University of Minnesota Press, 1983), p. 182.

16. Meredith Anne Skura, *The Literary Use of the Psychoanalytic Process* (New Haven: Yale University Press, 1981), pp. 79–80.

17. *kāmattiṉ iyal paṟiyāta vaṉkaṇṇar.* See *Kuṟuntokai*, ed. U. Vē. Cāminātaiyar (Aṇṇāmalainakar: Aṇṇāmalai-p-Palkalai-k-kaḻakam, 1983), p. 593.

18. See *The Study of Stolen Love: A Translation of Kaḷaviyal eṉṟa Iṟaiyaṉār Akapporuḷ with Commentary by Nakkīraṉār,* trans. David C. Buck and K. Paramasivam (Atlanta: Scholars Press, 1997).

19. An *antāti* is a composition of a hundred verses in which the last word, phrase, or line of the preceding verse forms the opening of the succeeding. *Purāṇas* are mytho-historical narratives; *piḷḷai-t-tamiḻs* are devotional compositions in which deities are addressed as children.

20. U. Vē. Cāminātaiyar, *Eṉ Carittiram* (Tiruvāṉmiyūr, Ceṉṉai: Ṭākṭar U. Vē. Cāminātaiyar Nūl Nilaiyam, 1980), p. 531.

21. An eighth-century narrative poem composed by Tiruttakkatēvar, a Jaina monk. The *Cīvaka Cintāmaṇi* is distinguished from *cañkam* poetry and grammar and the *Cilappatikāram* by a clear Jaina sectarian agenda in the text: in its final verses, the hero reaches omniscience at the feet of Mahāvīra himself.

22. Cāminātaiyar, *Eñ Carittiram,* pp. 555–556.

23. Ibid.

24. Ibid., pp. 723–724.

25. Ibid., p. 724.

26. Jagannathan, *Swaminatha Iyer,* p. 30.

27. I am certain that the translator, Jagannathan, means "erotic" rather than "romantic."

28. Ibid., p. 40.

29. Ibid., pp. 42–43.

30. Lyn E. Bigelow, personal communication, Chicago, February 1993.

Chapter 4: Reading the Sanskrit *Amaruśataka*

1. Siegfried Lienhard, *A History of Classical Poetry: Sanskrit/Pali/Prakit* (Wiesbaden: Otto Harrassowitz, 1984), p. 94.
2. Kane, *History of Sanskrit Poetics*, 4th ed. (New Delhi: Motilal Banarsidass, 1971), p. 166.
3. George C.O. Haas, introduction to *The "Daśarūpa": A Treatise on Hindu Dramaturgy by Dhanaṃjaya* (New York: AMS Press, 1965) p. xxxiii.
4. Kane, *History*, p. 274.
5. P. K. Gode, "The Commentary of Caturbhuja Miśra on the *Amaruśataka* and Its Chronology," in *Adyar Library Bulletin* (Madras: Adyar Library and Research Centre, 1943), 7:69–74. I should also note here that when I refer to a poem by number, I am using Arjunavarmadeva's recension. My English translations are also based on this version.
6. See Chintaman Ramchandra Devadhar's introduction to the *Amaruśatakam with the "Śṛṅgāradīpikā" of Vemabhūpāla* (New Delhi: Motilal Banarsidass, 1984), p. 30.
7. Haas, introduction, p. xxxvii.
8. Ingalls, introduction to *The "Dhvanyāloka" of Ānandavardhana with The Locana of Abhinavagupta*, trans. Daniel Ingalls, Jeffrey Masson, and M.V. Patwardhan (Cambridge: Harvard University Press, 1990), p. 13.
9. Ibid., p. 14.
10. Ibid.
11. Edwin Gerow, *A Glossary of Indian Figures of Speech* (The Hague: Mouton, 1971), p. 110.
12. See *Amaruśatakam* with the Sanskrit commentary *"Śṛṅgāra-dīpikā" of Vemabhūpāla*, critically edited with an introduction, English translation, and appendices by Chintaman Ramchandra Devadhar (New Delhi: Motilal Banarsidass, 1984), pp. 101–102.
13. *Amaruśatakam*, Vemabhūpāla's commentary, p. 14.
14. Ibid., pp. 46–47.
15. See *Amaruśatakam* with Arjunavarmadeva's commentary, p. 36.
16. Roland Barthes, *The Pleasure of the Text*, translated from French by Richard Miller (Oxford: Basil Blackwell, 1990), pp. 53–58.
17. Ānandavardhana, *Dhvanyāloka*, with the *Locana* of Abhina-

vagupta, and with Hindi paraphrase and commentary by Rāmsāgar Tripāthī (New Delhi: Motilal Banarsidass, 1982), 3:105.

18. *Amaruśatakam,* Arjunavarmadeva's commentary, p. 51. Arjunavarmadeva is probably quoting Dhanika's commentary on the *Daśarūpaka.* This verse is cited at *Daśarūpaka* 2.18 as an example of a *bhāva-pragalbhā-nāyikā* as a further articulation of Dhanañjaya's three-fold classification of the Sanskrit heroine as *mugdhā, madhyā,* or *pragalbhā;* "inexperienced, somewhat experienced, or experienced."

19. *Amaruśatakam,* Arjunavarmadeva's commentary, pp. 68–69. This poem resonates beautifully with standard mythological paradigms in the cycles of Kṛṣṇa, wherein he replicates himself in such a way that Kaṃsa, his evil uncle (or cousin), sees him in whichever direction he looks, and, needless to say, provides endless copies of himself as the cowherd lover in the *rāsamaṇḍala.*

20. *Amaruśatakam,* Vemabhūpāla's commentary, p. 97.

21. *Amaruśatakam,* Arjunavarmadeva's commentary, p. 53.

22. Roland Barthes, pleasure, p. 57.

23. Ibid., p. 58.

Chapter 5: Reading the Prākit *Gāthās*

1. Siegfried Lienhard, *A History of Classical Poetry: Sanskrit/Pali/Prakit* (Wiesbaden: Otto Harrassowitz, 1984), p. 80.

2. George Hart, *The Poems of Ancient Tamil: Their Milieu and Their Sanskrit Counterparts* (Berkeley: University of California Press, 1975), pp. 3–4.

3. Lienhard, *Classical Poetry,* p. 84.

4. See, for example, A. K. Warder's characterization of the *Gāthāsaptaśatī* in *Indian Kāvya Literature* (New Delhi: Motilal Banarsidass, 1972–1988), 2:189.

5. Arthur Berriedale Keith, *Classical Sanskrit Literature* (Calcutta: Y.M.C.A. Publishing House, 1958), pp. 6–8.

6. Ibid., pp. 98–99.

7. I would suggest that the *gāthā* was most likely the inspiration for the Sanskrit poem.

8. Michael Riffaterre, *Semiotics of Poetry* (Bloomington: Indiana University Press, 1978), p. 27.

9. Ibid., p. 170.

10. Dhanika, commentator on Dhanañjaya's *Daśarūpa,* cites verses from the *Gāthāsaptaśatī* in eight separate instances, but in a cursory and

an uninteresting way. I have chosen not to include examples from his commentary here.

11. Meredith Anne Skura, *The Literary Use of the Psychoanalytic Process* (New Haven: Yale University Press, 1981), p. 126.

12. Harold Bloom, *Sigmund Freud's "The Interpretation of Dreams"* (New York: Chelsea House, 1987), p. 3.

13. Daniel H.H. Ingalls, introduction to *The "Dhvanyāloka" of Ānandavardhana with the "Locana" of Abhinavagupta,* trans. Daniel Ingalls, Jeffrey Masson, and M.V. Patwardhan (Cambridge: Harvard University Press, 1990), p. 5.

14. Ibid., p. 13.

15. Michael Riffaterre, *Semiotics of Poetry* (Bloomington: Indiana University Press, 1978), p. 35.

16. Dr. R. N. Sampath, personal communication, Madras, February 1989.

17. See, for instance, his commentary on verse 1.13.

Chapter 6: Conclusion

1. Romila Thapar, "A Historical Perspective on the Story of Rāma," in *Anatomy of a Confrontation: Ayodhyā and the Rise of Communal Politics in India,* ed. Sarvepalli Gopal (London: Zed, 1993), p. 143.

2. Ibid., p. 150.

3. Ibid., p. 158.

4. See my discussion of *Naṟṟiṇai* 110 in chapter 1. In the translations that follow I have included a set of poems from the *caṅkam* tradition exclusively composed on the theme of the mother's voice in the context of separation.

5. David Halperin, John J. Winkler, and Froma I. Zeitlin, eds., *Before Sexuality: The Construction of Erotic Experience in the Ancient Greek World* (Princeton: Princeton University Press, 1990), pp. 3–20.

6. See, for example, *Naṟṟiṇai* 45, quoted in chapter 3.

7. I thank Robert P. Goldman for drawing my attention to certain poems in this text.

8. A. K. Warder, *Indian Kāvya Literature* (New Delhi: Motilal Banarsidass, 1972–1988), 5:81.

9. Siegfried Lienhard, *A History of Classical Poetry: Sanskrit/Pali/Prakit* (Wiesbaden: Otto Harrassowitz, 1984), p. 87.

10. See M. V. Patwardhan's introduction to *Jayavallabha's Vajjālaggaṃ* (Ahmedabad: Prakrit Text Society, 1969), p. xii.

11. Warder, *Kāvya Literature,* 5:82.

12. Patwardhan, *Vajjālaggaṃ,* p. xlvii.

13. Ibid., p. 516.

14. Paul Smith, "Vas," in *Feminisms: An Anthology of Literary Theory and Criticism,* ed. Robyn R. Warhol and Diane Price Herndl (New Brunswick: Rutgers University Press, 1991), p. 1011.

15. Ibid., p. 1020.

16. Ibid., p. 1015.

17. Margaret Trawick, "Wandering Lost: A Landless Laborer's Sense of Place and Self," in *Gender, Genre, and Power in South Asian Expressive Traditions,* ed. Arjun Appadurai, Frank J. Korom, and Margaret A. Mills (Philadelphia: University of Pennsylvania Press, 1991), p. 246.

Bibliography

Abhinavagupta. *Dhvanyāloka-Locana*. With an anonymous Sanskrit commentary. *Uddyota* 1. Critically edited with English translation by K. Krishnamoorthy. New Delhi: Meharchand Lachhmandas Publications, 1988.

Aiṅkuṟunūṟu Mūlamum Paḷaiyavuraiyum. Edited by U. Vē. Cāminātaiyar. Ceṉṉai: Ṭākṭar U. Vē. Cāminātaiyar Nūl Nilaiyam, 1980.

Aiṅkuṟunūṟu, the Short Five Hundred. Translated with introduction and notes by P. Jotimuttu. Madras: Christian Literature Society, 1984.

Aiṅkuṟunūṟu. Ceṉṉai: Es. Rājam, 1958.

Amaruka. *Das Amarucataka in seiner Recensionen dargestellt mit einer Einleitung und Auszugen aus den Commentatoren versehen*. By Richard Simon. Kiel: C. F. Haeseler Verlag für Orientalische Literatur, 1893.

———. *Amaruśatakam*. Edited by Vidyanivas Misra. Delhi: Rajakamal Prakasan, 1965.

———. *Amaruśatakam*. With the Sanskrit commentary "Rasikasañjīvinī" of Arjunavarmadeva. New Delhi: Motilal Banarsidass, 1983.

———. *Amaruśatakam*. With the Sanskrit commentary "Śṛṅgāradīpikā" of Vemabhūpāla. Critically edited with an introduction, English translation, and appendices by Chintaman Ramchandra Devadhar. 1959. Reprint, New Delhi: Motilal Banarsidass, 1984.

———. *Dhvanyāloka*. With "Locana" of Abhinavagupta. With Hindi paraphrase and commentary by Rāmsāgar Tripāṭhī. 2d ed. 3 vols. New Delhi: Motilal Banarsidass, 1981.

———. Ānandavardhana. *Dhvanyāloka by Ānandavardhana and Locana by Abhinavagupta*. With "Kaumudī" by Uttuṅgodaya and "Upalocana" by Kuppusvāmi Śāstri. *Uddyota* 1. Edited by S. Kuppuswami Sastri, T. V. Ramachandra Diksitar, and T. R. Chintamani. Madras: Kuppuswami Sastri Research Institute, 1944.

———. *Dhvanyāloka of Ānandavardhana*. Critically edited with introduction, English translation, and notes by K. Krishnamoorthy. Dharwar: Karnatak University, 1974.

———. *The Dhvanyāloka of Ānandavardhana.* With the "Locana" of Abhinavagupta. Translated by Daniel H. H. Ingalls, Jeffrey Moussaieff Masson, and M. V. Patwardhan. Edited and with an introduction by Daniel H. H. Ingalls. Cambridge: Harvard University Press, 1990.

Ananthanarayana, Hallimysore Suryanarayana. *A Prākrit Reader: A Linguistic Introduction Based on Selections from Hāla's Sattasaī*. Mysore: Central Institute of Indian Languages, 1973.

Aristotle. *The Poetics of Aristotle.* Translation and commentary by Stephen Halliwell. Chapel Hill: University of North Carolina Press, 1987.

Arumugham, K. *A Critical Study of Naccinārkkiniyar.* Madras: University of Madras, 1981.

Auerbach, Erich. *Mimesis: The Representation of Reality in Western Literature.* Translated from German by Willard Trask. Garden City, N.Y.: Doubleday, 1957.

Bachelard, Gaston. *The Poetics of Space.* Translated from French by Maria Joles with a foreword by Etienne Gilson. Boston: Beacon, 1969.

Barthes, Roland. "The World As Object." In *A Barthes Reader.* Edited with an introduction by Susan Sontag. New York: Hill and Wang, 1982.

———. *The Pleasure of the Text.* Translated from French by Richard Miller. Oxford: Basil Blackwell, 1990.

Baumer, Rachel van M., and James R. Brandon, eds. *Sanskrit Drama in Performance.* Honolulu: University of Hawaii Press, 1981.

Benveniste, Emile. *Problems in General Linguistics.* Translated from French by Mary Elizabeth Meek. Coral Gables, Fla.: University of Miami Press, 1971.

Bharata Muni. *Nāṭyaśāstra.* Edited by Paṇḍit Śivadatta and Kāśīnāth Pāṇḍuraṅg Parab. *Kāvyamālā*, no. 42. Bombay: Nirṇaya Sāgara Press, 1894.

———. *Nāṭyaśāstra.* With the commentary of Abhinavagupta. Gaekwad's Oriental Series, no. 68. Baroda: Oriental Institute, 1934

———. *Nāṭyaśāstra.* With the commentary "Abhinavabharati" by Abhinavaguptācārya. 4 vols. Edited with an introduction by R. S. Nagar. New Delhi: Parimal, 1981.

———. *The Nāṭya Śāstra of Bharatamuni.* Translated into English by "A Board of Scholars." Rāga Nṛtya Series, no. 2. New Delhi: Sri Satguru Publications, 1990.

Bhojarāja. *Sarasvatīkaṇṭhābharaṇa of Śrī Bhojadeva.* With the commentary "Hṛdayahāriṇī" of Nārāyaṇa Daṇḍanātha. Edited by V. A. Ramaswami Sastri. Trivandrum: Superintendent, Government Press, 1948.

Bloom, Harold, ed. *Sigmund Freud's "The Interpretation of Dreams."* New York: Chelsea, 1987.

Borooah, Anundoram. *Prosody.* Gauhati: Publication Board of Assam, 1975.

Cāminātaiyar, U. Vē. *The Story of My Life.* Translated from Tamil by S. K. Guruswamy and edited by A. Rama Iyer. Tiruvāṉmiyūr, Ceṉṉai: Ṭākṭar U. Vē. Cāminātaiyar Nūl Nilaiyam, 1980.

———. *Eṉ Carittiram.* 2d ed. Tiruvāṉmiyūr, Ceṉṉai: Tāṭkar U. Vē. Cāminātaiyar Nūl Nilaiyam, 1982.

Chawaf, Chantal. "Linguistic Flesh." In *New French Feminisms: An Anthology.* Edited by Elaine Marks and Isabelle de Courtivron. New York: Schocken, 1982.

Chettiar, A. Chidambaranatha. *Advanced Studies in Tamil Prosody (Being a History of Tamil Prosody up to the Tenth Century A.D.).* Annamalainagar: Annamalai University, 1957.

Colomina, Beatriz, ed. *Sexuality and Space.* New York: Princeton Architectural Press, 1992.

Crane, Robert Salmon. *The Languages of Criticism and the Structure of Poetry.* Toronto: University of Toronto Press, 1953.

Culler, Jonathan. "Literary Competence." In *Reader-Response Criticism: From Formalism to Structuralism.* Edited by Jane P. Tompkins. Baltimore: Johns Hopkins University Press, 1980.

———. *On Deconstruction: Theory and Criticism after Structuralism.* Ithaca, N.Y.: Cornell University Press, 1982.

Cutler, Norman. *Songs of Experience: The Poetics of Tamil Devotion.* Bloomington: Indiana University Press, 1987.

Dhanañjaya. *The Daśarūpa, or Hindu Canons of Dramaturgy.* With the exposition of Dhanika, the "Avaloka." Edited by Fitz-edward Hall. D.C.L. Fasciculus 1. Calcutta: Baptist Mission Press, 1861.

———. *The Daśarūpaka of Dhanañjaya.* With the commentary of Dhanika and "Daśarūpa" from the *Bhāratīya Nāṭyaśāstra.* Edited by Kāśīnāth Pāṇḍuraṅg Parab. 5th ed. Bombay: Nirṇaya Sāgara Press, 1941.

———. *The Daśarūpa: A Treatise on Hindu Dramaturgy.* Translated from Sanskrit with an introduction by George C.O. Haas. New York: AMS Press, 1965.

Dimock, Edward Cameron, et al. *The Literatures of India: An Introduction*. Chicago: University of Chicago Press, 1974.

Dundas, Paul. "The *Sattsaī* and Its Commentators." In *Indologica Taurinensia*. Vol. 17. Torino: Instituto di Indologia, 1985.

Eagleton, Terry. *Literary Theory: An Introduction*. Minneapolis: University of Minnesota Press, 1983.

Eco, Umberto. *The Role of the Reader: Explorations in the Semiotics of Texts*. Bloomington: Indiana University Press, 1984.

———. *Travels in Hyperreality*. San Diego: Harcourt, Brace and Jovanovich, 1986.

Elayaperumal, M. *Grammar of Aiǵkurunuuru with Index*. Trivandrum: University of Kerala, 1975.

Fabricius, J. P. *Tamil and English Dictionary*. 4th ed. Tranquebar: Evangelical Lutheran Mission Publishing House, 1972.

Foucault, Michel. *The History of Sexuality*. Vol. 1,: *An Introduction*. New York: Random House, 1980.

Freud, Sigmund. *The Interpretation of Dreams*. Translated by Dr. A. A. Brill. New York: Modern Library, 1950.

———. *Beyond the Pleasure Principle*. Translated by James Strachey. With an introduction and notes by Dr. Gregory Zilboorg. New York: Bantam, 1959.

Frye, Northrop. *Anatomy of Criticism*. Princeton: Princeton University Press, 1957.

Gerow, Edwin Mahaffey. *A Glossary of Indian Figures of Speech*. The Hague: Mouton, 1971.

———. "*Rasa* as a Category of Literary Criticism: What Are the Limits of Its Application?" In *Sanskrit Drama in Performance*. Edited by Rachel van M. Baumer and James R. Brandon. Honolulu: The University Press of Hawaii, 1981.

Gilbert, Sandra M. "What Do Feminist Critics Want? A Postcard from the Volcano." In *The New Feminist Criticism: Essays on Women, Literature and Theory*. Edited by Elaine Showalter. New York: Pantheon, 1985.

Gode, P. K. "The Commentary of Caturbhuja Miśra of Kāmpilya on the *Amaruśataka* and Its Chronology." In *Adyar Library Bulletin*. Vol. 7. Madras: The Adyar Library and Research Centre, 1943.

Hāla. *Das Saptaçatakam des Hāla*. Edited by Albrecht Weber. Leipzig: F. A. Brockhaus, 1881.

———. *The Gāthāsaptaśatī of Sātavāhana*. With the commentary of Gaṅgādharabhaṭṭa. Edited by Paṇḍit Durgāprasād and Kāśīnāth

Paṇḍuraṅg Parab. *Kāvyamālā*, no. 21. Bombay: Nirṇaya Sāgara Press, 1889.

———. *Haritāmrapītāmbara's Gāthāsaptāśatī prakāśika: A Hitherto Unpublished Commentary on Hāla's Gāthāsaptāśatī, IV–VII Śatakas.* Edited with a critical introduction by Jagdish Lal Shastri. Lahore: N.p., 1942.

———. *Gāthāsaptaśatī*. Edited with introduction and Hindi commentary by Paramānanda Śāstrī. Merat: Prakāśan Pratisthan, 1965.

———. *Gāthāsaptaśatī (Gāhāsattasaī).* Kāśī Saṃskṛta Granthamālā, no. 192. Vārāṇasī: Caukhamba Sanskrit Series Office, 1969.

———. *The Prākrit Gāthāsaptaśatī, compiled by Sātavāhana King Hāla.* Edited with an introduction and English translation by Radhagovind Basak. Bibliotheca Indica, no. 295. Calcutta: Asiatic Society, 1971.

———. *Hāla's Gāhākoṣa (Gāthāsaptāśatī) with the Sanskrit Commentary of Bhuvanapāla.* Vol. 1. Edited by M. V. Patwardhan. Prākrit Text Series, no. 21. Ahmedabad: Prākrit Text Society, 1980.

———. *Gāthāsaptāśatī of Sātavāhana Hāla.* With Sanskrit *chāyā* and commentary by Bhaṭṭa Mathurānāth Śāstrī. 1933. Reprint, New Delhi: Motilal Banarsidass, 1983.

———. *The Gāhākoṣa of Hāla, Part II.* Edited with an introduction, translation, index of stanzas, glossary, and notes by M. V. Patwardhan. New Delhi: B. L. Institute of Indology, 1988.

———. *The Absent Traveller: Prākrit Love Poetry from the Gāthāsaptaśatī of Sātavāhana Hāla.* Selected and translated by Arvind Krishna Mehrotra. New Delhi: Ravi Dayal, 1991.

Halperin, David M., John J. Winkler, and Froma I. Zeitlin, eds. *Before Sexuality: The Construction of the Erotic Experience in the Ancient Greek World.* Princeton: Princeton University Press, 1990.

Hart, George L. *The Poems of Ancient Tamil: Their Milieu and Their Sanskrit Counterparts.* Berkeley: University of California Press, 1975.

———. "The Relation between Tamil and Classical Sanskrit Literature." In *A History of Indian Literature.* Vol. 10, *Dravidian Literature,* fascicle 2. Wiesbaden: Harrassowitz, 1976.

Index des Mots de la Litterature Tamoule Ancienne. 3 vols. Publications de l'Institut Français d'Indologie, no. 37. Pondicherry: Institut Français d'Indologie, 1967–70.

I̱raiyaṉār. *The Study of Stolen Love: A Translation of Kaḷaviyal eṉṟa*

Iṟaiyaṉār Akapporuḷ with Commentary by Nakkīraṉār. Translated with an introduction by David C. Buck and K. Paramasivam. Atlanta: Scholars Press, 1997.

Jagannathan, K. V. *U. V. Swaminatha Iyer.* New Delhi: Sahitya Akademi, 1987.

Jayavallabha, comp. *Jayavallabha's Vajjālaggaṃ* . With an introduction and English translation by M. V. Patwardhan. Ahmedabad: Prākrit Text Society, 1969.

Jesudasan, C., and Hephzibah Jesudasan. *A History of Tamil Literature.* Calcutta: Y.M.C.A. Publishing House, 1961.

Jones, Ernest. "The Symbolic Significance of Salt in Folklore and Superstition." In *Essays in Applied Psycho-Analysis.* London: International Psycho-Analytical Press, 1923.

Kane, P. V. *History of Sanskrit Poetics*. 4th ed. New Delhi: Motilal Banarsidass, 1987.

Keith, Arthur Berriedale. *Classical Sanskrit Literature.* London: Oxford University Press, 1923.

Krishnambal, S. R. *Grammar of Kuṟuntokai with Index.* Trivandrum: University of Kerala, 1974.

Kulkarni, V. M., ed. *Prakrit Verses in Sanskrit Works on Poetics.* Vol. 1. New Delhi: Bhogilal Leherchand Institute of Indology, 1988.

Kundera, Milan. *The Art of the Novel.* New York: Grove, 1988.

Kuṟuntokai. *The Interior Landscape: Love Poems from a Classical Tamil Anthology.* Translated by A. K. Ramanujan. Bloomington: Indiana University Press, 1967.

———. *Kuṟuntokai: An Anthology of Classical Tamil Love Poetry.* Translated by M. Shanmugam Pillai and David E. Ludden. Madurai: Koodal Publishers, 1976.

———. Edited with commentary by Po. Vē. Cōmacuntaraṉār. Ceṉṉai: Tirunelvēli Teṉṉintiya Caivacittānta Nūṟpatippuk-k-Kaḻakam Limiṭeṭ, 1978.

———. Edited with commentary by U. Vē. Cāminātaiyar. Aṇṇāmlainakar: Aṇṇāmalai-p-Palkalai-k-Kaḻakam, 1983.

Lacan, Jacques. *Écrits: A Selection.* Translated from French by Alan Sheridan. New York: Norton, 1977.

———. *The Four Fundamental Concepts of Psycho-Analysis.* Edited by Jacques-Alain Miller. Translated from French by Alan Sheridan. New York: Norton, 1981.

———. *Feminine Sexuality: Jacques Lacan and the "École Freudienne."* Edited by Juliet Mitchell and Jacqueline Rose. Translated from

French by Jacqueline Rose. New York: W. W. Norton and Company, 1985.

Lienhard, Siegfried. *A History of Classical Poetry: Sanskrit/Pali/Prakrit.* Wiesbaden: Harrassowitz, 1984.

Love Poems of Ancient India. Selected and translated by K. S. Srinivasan. New Delhi: Rasika Trust, 1988.

Mammaṭa. *Kāvyaprakāśa.* With the commentary "Bālabodhinī" by Vamanacharya Ramabhatta Jhalkikar. Edited by Raghunath Damodar Karmarkar. Poona: Bhandarkar Oriental Research Institute, 1965.

———. *The Poetic Light: Kāvyaprakāśa of Mammaṭa.* With the commentary "Sampradāyaprakāśinī" of Śrīvidyācakravartin. Translated by R. C. Dwivedi. 2 vols. New Delhi: Motilal Banarsidass, 1977.

———. *Kāvyaprakāśa.* With commentary by Śivarāja. New Delhi: Motilal Banarsidass, 1980.

Marr, John Ralston. *The Eight Anthologies: A Study in Early Tamil Literature.* Tiruvanmiyur, Madras: Institute of Asian Studies, 1985.

Masson, J. L., and M. V. Patwardhan. *Aesthetic Rapture: The Rasādhyāya of the Nāṭyaśāstra.* 2 vols. Poona: Deccan College Postgraduate and Research Institute, 1970.

Meenakshisundaram, T. P. *A History of Tamil Literature.* Annamalainagar: Annamalai University, 1965.

Miner, Earl. "Some Theoretical and Methodological Topics for Comparative Literature." *Poetics Today* 8, no. 1 (1987).

———. *Comparative Poetics: An Intercultural Essay on Theories of Literature.* Princeton: Princeton University Press, 1990.

Mitra, Arati. *Origin and Development of Sanskrit Metrics.* Calcutta: Asiatic Society, 1989.

Mukherji, Amulyadhan. *Sanskrit Prosody: Its Evolution.* Calcutta: Saraswat Library, 1976.

Narriṇai. Cennai: Es. Rājam, 1957.

Naṟṟiṇai Nāṉūṟu. With commentary and exegesis by A. Nārāyaṇcāmi Aiyar and grammatical exposition by Po. Vē. Cōmacuntaraṉār. Reprint of the 3d ed. Ceṉṉai: Tirunelvēli Teṉṉintiya Caivacittānta Nūṟpatippu-k-Kaḻakam, Limiṭeṭ, 1976.

Paramasivam, K. "Relative Chronology of *Tolkāppiyam* and Early Sangam." In *Studies in Dravidian Linguistics.* Edited by S. Vaidyanatham and Jardiljeet Singh Sidhu. Pakha Sanjam, vol. 10. Patiala: Panjabi University, 1980. *Studies in Dravidian Linguistics.*

Pavaṇanti. *Naṉṉūl.* With commentary by Kūḻarikaittampirāṉ. Edited by A. Dhamotharan. Wiesbaden: Franz Steiner Verlag, 1980.

Periakaruppan, Ramasamy. *Tradition and Talent in Cañkam Poetry.* Madurai: Madurai Publishing House, 1976.

Peterson, Indira Viswanathan. *Poems to Śiva: The Hymns of the Tamil Saints.* Princeton: Princeton University Press, 1989.

Poems of Love and War: From the Eight Anthologies and the Ten Long Poems of Classical Tamil. Selected and translated by A. K. Ramanujan. New York: Columbia University Press, 1985.

Poets of the Tamil Anthologies: Ancient Poems of Love and War. Translated by George L. Hart III. Princeton: Princeton University Press, 1979.

Poulet, Georges. "Criticism and the Experience of Interiority." In *Reader-Response Criticism: From Formalism to Structuralism.* Edited by Jane P. Tompkins. Baltimore: Johns Hopkins University Press, 1980.

Puṟanāṉūṟu. Edited with commentary by U. Vē. Cāminātaiyar. Tañcāvūr: Tamiḻ-p-Palkalai-k-Kaḻakam, 1985. Reprint of the 6th ed.

Raghavan, V. *Śṛṅgāramañjarī of Saint Akbar Shah.* Hyderabad: Hyderabad Archaeological Department, Hyderabad Government, 1951.

Raja, K. Kunjunni. *Indian Theories of Meaning.* Madras: Adyar Library and Research Centre, 1963.

Rajam, V. S. *A Reference Grammar of Classical Tamil Poetry.* Philadelphia: American Philosophical Society, 1992.

Ramanujan, A. K. "Classics Lost and Found." In *Contemporary Indian Tradition: Voices on Culture, Nature, and the Challenge of Change.* Edited by Carla M. Borden. Washington, D.C.: Smithsonian Institution Press, 1989.

Riffaterre, Michael. *Text Production.* Translated from French by Terese Lyons. New York: Columbia University Press, 1983.

———. *Semiotics of Poetry.* Bloomington: Indiana University Press, 1984.

Rousselle, Aline. *Porneia: On Desire and the Body in Antiquity.* Translated from French by Felicia Pheasant. Oxford: Basil Blackwell, 1988.

Sanskrit Love Poetry. Translated by W. S. Merwin and J. Moussaieff Masson with an introduction by J. Moussaieff Masson. New York: Columbia University Press, 1977.

Sanskrit Poetry from Vidyākara's "Treasury." Compiled by Vidyākara. Translated with an introduction and notes by Daniel H. H. Ingalls. Cambridge: Harvard University Press, Belknap Press, 1965.

Saptaśatīsāra with Bhāvadīpikā of Vema Bhūpāla. With the *Chappaṇṇaya-Gāhāo* (text and *chāyā*). Edited by A. N. Upadhye. Shivaji University Sanskrit and Prākrit Series, vol. 3. Kolhapur: Shivaji University, 1970.

Saussure, Ferdinand de. *Course in General Linguistics.* New York: Philosophical Library, 1959.

Schwartzberg, Joseph E., ed. *A Historical Atlas of South Asia.* Chicago: University of Chicago Press, 1978.

Sharma, Ram Karan. *Elements of Poetry in the Mahābhārata.* 2d ed. New Delhi: Motilal Banarsidass, 1988.

Showalter, Elaine, ed. *The New Feminist Criticism: Essays on Women, Literature, and Theory.* New York: Pantheon, 1985.

Skura, Meredith Anne. *The Literary Use of the Psychoanalytic Process.* New Haven: Yale University Press, 1981.

Smith, David. "Classical Sanskrit Poetry and the Modern Reader." In *Contributions to South Asian Studies.* Vol. 2. Edited by Gopal Krishna. New Delhi: Oxford University Press, 1982.

Smith, Paul. "Vas." In *Feminisms: An Anthology of Literary Theory and Criticism.* Edited by Robyn R. Warhol and Diane Price Herndl. New Brunswick: Rutgers University Press, 1991.

Srinivasan, K. S. *The Ethos of Indian Literature: A Study of Its Romantic Tradition.* New Delhi: Chanakya Publications, 1985.

Stein, Burton. *Peasant, State, and Society in Medieval South India.* New York: Oxford University Press, 1980.

Steiner, George. *After Babel: Aspects of Language and Translation.* New York: Oxford University Press, 1975.

Strand, Mark. *The Monument.* New York: Ecco, 1978.

The Subhāṣitaratnakoṣa. Compiled by Vidyākara. Edited by D. D. Kosambi and V. V. Gokhale with an introduction by D. D. Kosambi. Harvard Oriental Series, vol. 42. Edited by Daniel H.H. Ingalls. Cambridge: Harvard University Press, 1957.

Subrahmanian, N. *Pre-Pallavan Tamil Index.* Madras: University of Madras, 1966.

Subramoniam, V. I. *Index of Pu̱ranaaṉuuṟu.* Trivandrum: University of Kerala, 1962.

Suleiman, Susan R. and Inge Crosman, eds. *The Reader in the Text: Essays on Audience and Interpretation.* Princeton: Princeton University Press, 1980.

Takahashi, Takanobu. *Tamil Love Poetry and Poetics.* Leiden: Brill, 1995.

Tēvāram: Hymnes Śivaïtes du Pays Tamoul. Edited by T. V. Gopal Iyer. 2 vols. Pondichéry: Institut Français d'Indologie, 1984–1985.

Thapar, Romila. "A Historical Perspective on the Story of Rāma." In *Anatomy of a Confrontation: Ayodhyā and the Rise of Communal Politics in India.* Edited by Sarvepalli Gopal. London: Zed, 1993.

Tieken, Herman. "A Formal Type of Arrangement in the Vulgata of the *Gāthasāptaśatī* of Hāla." *Studien zur Indologie und Iranistik,* vol. 4. Edited by Oskar von Hinüber, Gert Klingenschmitt, Albrecht Wezler, and Michael Witzel. Reinbek: Verlage für orientalistische Fachpublikationen, 1978.

Tirugnanasambandhan, P. *The Concepts of Alamkara Sastra in Tamil.* Madras: Samskrita Academy, 1977.

Todorov, Tzvetan. *The Fantastic: A Structural Approach to a Literary Genre.* Translated from French by Richard Howard with a foreword by Robert Scholes. Ithaca, N.Y.: Cornell University Press, 1975.

———. *Introduction to Poetics.* Translated from French by Richard Howard. Introduction by Peter Brooks. Minneapolis: University of Minnesota Press, 1981.

———. *Theories of the Symbol.* Translated from French by Catherine Porter. Ithaca, N.Y.: Cornell University Press, 1982.

Tolkāppiyaṉār. *Tolkāppiyam-Poruḷatikāram.* Translated into English by E. S. Varadaraja Iyer. Annamalainagar: Annamalai University, 1948.

———. *Tolkāppiyam: The Earliest Extant Tamil Grammar: Text in Tamil and Roman Scripts with a Critical Commentary in English.* English translation and commentary by P. S. Subrahmanya Sastri. Parts 1–3, "*Poruḷatikāram:* Tamil Poetics." Madras: Kuppuswami Sastri Research Institute, 1959, 1952, 1956.

———. *Tholkāppiyam in English with Critical Studies.* English translation and notes by S. Ilakkuvanar. Madurai: Kural Neri Publishing House, 1963.

———. *Tolkāppiyam.* Madurai: Cittārtta Publishing House, 1978.

———. *Tolkāppiyam: Poruḷatikāram.* Edited by Ku. Cuntaramūrtti. With the commentaries of Nacciṉārkkiṉiyar and Pērāciriyar. 3 vols. Aṇṇāmalainakar: Aṇṇāmalai-p-Palkalai-k-Kaḻakam, 1985–1986.

———. *Tolkāppiyam: Poruḷatikāram.* With the commentary of Iḷampūraṇar. 3 vols. Ceṉṉai: Tirunelvēli Teṉṉintiya Caiva Cittānta Nūṟpatippu-k-Kaḻakam Limiṭeṭ, 1986.

Trawick, Margaret. "Wandering Lost: A Landless Laborer's Sense of Place and Self." In *Gender, Genre, and Power in South Asian Expressive Traditions.* Edited by Arjun Appadurai, Frank J. Korom, and Margaret A. Mills. Philadelphia: University of Pennsylvania Press, 1991.

Varadarajan, Mu. *A History of Tamil Literature.* Translated from Tamil by E. Sa. Visswanathan. New Delhi: Sahitya Akademi, 1988.

Vātsyāyana. *Kāmasūtram.* With the Jayamaṅgalā Sanskrit commentary of Śrī Yaśodhara. Edited with Hindi Commentary by Śrī Devduṭṭa Śāstrī. Varanasi: Chaukhambha Sanskrit Sansthan, 1982.

Warder, A. K. *Indian Kāvya Literature.* 6 vols. New Delhi: Motilal Banarsidass, 1972.

Winternitz, Moriz. *A History of Indian Literature.* Translated from German by Mrs. S. Ketkar. Calcutta: University of Calcutta, 1927–1960.

Zvelebil, Kamil. *The Smile of Murugan on Tamil Literature of South India.* Leiden: Brill, 1973.

———. *Tamil Literature.* In *A History of Indian Literature.* Vol. 10, *Dravidian Literatures*, fascicle 1. Wiesbaden: Harrassowitz, 1974.

———. *Literary Conventions in Akam Poetry.* Tiruvanmiyur, Madras: Institute of Asian Studies, 1986.

———. *Classical Tamil Prosody: An Introduction.* Madras: New Era Publications, 1989.

Index